When he came to our house, Andy espied a monograph
on Kurt Schwitters and spontaneously embarked on a
performance of the *Ur Sonata*. I was entranced as was our
dog, who clearly connected to the intermittent baying.
Andy has made this extraordinary piece central to his
repertoire, and this memoir recounts vividly his joURney
with it, while offering a rich and insightful account of
Schwitters' own. The reader will embrace and improvise
on the marvelous array of phonetic murmurations and be
the better for it.

—H. Nichols B. Clark, Founding Director and Chief
Curator Emeritus, Eric Carle Museum of Picture Book
Art

Praise for *The Music Thief*:

A lucid and wise coming-of-age memoir, in which the author searches for himself in the worlds of improvisational theater, free jazz, and Black liberation. But his explorations lead to a head-on collision with reality when he hears someone yelling, 'Help, murder! Help! They're killing me!'

> —Seth Tobocman, *You Don't Have to Fuck People Over to Survive;* co-founder *World War 3 Illustrated*

Praise for *Rebel Bookseller: Why Indie Businesses Represent Everything You Want to Fight For—From Free Speech to Buying Local to Building Communities:*

Laties is witty, opinionated for sure, impassioned, but eminently practical in both his desires for independent bookselling and how to actually do it effectively. Activists of all stripes, not just booksellers, can learn from this book. It made me laugh. It made me think. It inspired me. It'll do the same for you too.

> —Ramsey Kanaan, co-founder AK Press and PM Press

Praise for *Son of Rebel Bookseller:*

Interlaced with the vivid imaginative writing Samuel Laties composed throughout his short life, *Son of Rebel Bookseller* is a testament to a father's love for his son and a chronicle of the search for meaning after devastating loss.

> —Lee Upton, *The Tao of Humiliation: Stories*

Ur Sonata, recited by Andrew Laties (*Ur Sonata* text is taped up onto back wall). Cabaret Voltaire, Chicago. June 1988.
Photo by Ed Sacks.

LIVING
UR SONATA

plus

UR SONATA

LIVING UR SONATA

conjuring kurt schwitters to transcend authority and seize the hour

by andrew laties

plus

UR SONATA

or, lautsonate, phonetic sonata, portrait of raoul hausmann, primeval sonata, sonata in primeval sounds, sonate in urlauten, sonate présyllabique, urlaut-sonate, ursonate

by kurt schwitters

The events and conversations in this book have been set down to the best of the author's ability.

Published by Mythoprint Publishing, Easton, PA, USA, 18042
Library of Congress Control Number: 2023941791
ISBN 978-1-953465-04-7 (pbk.) ISBN 978-1-953465-05-4 (ebook)

Laties, Andrew, author. Schwitters, Kurt, author.
 Living ur sonata, conjuring kurt schwitters to transcend authority and seize the hour, plus ur sonata, or, lautsonate, phonetic sonata, portrait of raoul hausmann, primeval sonata, sonata in primeval sounds, sonate in urlauten, sonate présyllabique, urlaut-sonate, ursonate / Andrew Laties / Kurt Schwitters

1.   Schwitters, Kurt. 2. Ursonate. 3. Dadaism. 4. Merz. 5. Avant-garde (Music). 6. Poetry—Nonsense. 7. German literature—Literary history and criticism. 8. Art History—Modern. 9. Laties, Andrew. I. Title.

Cover design by Rebecca Migdal.
Cover photo by Peter Palombella, Holyoke 2009: Andrew Laties, Rebecca Migdal, Eric Blitz, in front of the painting "Dream of the Dying Ones," by Rebecca Migdal.
Cover photos of Kurt Schwitters: Ernst Schwitters, *Kurt Schwitters beim Vortrag seiner Urlaut-Sonate*. London. 1944. © 2023 Artists Rights Society (ARS), New York / VG Bild-Kunst, Bonn (also courtesy Kurt Schwitters Archive, Sprengel Museum, Hannover).
Kurt Schwitters photos appear here on book-jacket (designed by Naomi Yang) of: Kurt Schwitters, *PPPPPP: Poems Performances Pieces Proses Plays Poetics*, edited & translated by Jerome Rothenberg & Pierre Joris. Cambridge, MA: Exact Change, 2002.

Printed and bound in the United States of America
First printing August 1, 2023

For Rebecca

CONTENTS

PREFACE

The general sense of insecurity was expressed in growing levels of violence and bigotry. Vicious skirmishes between political opponents were common. The calls for a strong leader to take command grew louder. Thus the culture of the Weimar period, which had stood for democracy, for internationalism and for a new order, started to founder even before 1933. A massive backwash of resentment was building up in Germany, against the government, against foreign influences and against a perceived breakdown of traditional values. When the surge of reaction hit the arts, it swept aside the whole edifice—Constructivism and topless revues, Thomas Mann and Tarzan of the Apes, Bert Brecht and Josephine Baker alike.

–Gwendolen Webster, *Kurt Merz Schwitters*

SCHWITTERS CRACKS UP HITLER

A century ago—between World War I and World War II—the artist Kurt Schwitters spent ten years developing an unusual nonsense poem. He gave dozens of recitals, in Germany, Czechoslovakia, Holland, and Switzerland, then later in Norway and England. His poem grew and changed with every performance. He invented a method for transcribing the piece, and self-published a thousand copies.

In that era of resurgent nationalism, Schwitters was a pacifist and Utopian supranationalist: he opposed the idea of nation-states. In 1924 he wrote, "Anyone who is supranational cannot understand the hatred that nations have for each other."

Schwitters could get along in several languages; he understood that people are divided by language. Our mother tongue is a mechanism for internalizing our nation's prejudices, clichés, metaphors, knee-jerk associations, and lies. We are polluted from our earliest years with baked-in historical agendas. Someone who does not speak my language may be my enemy.

In writing about his sound-poetry Schwitters announced his personal mission to free words and letters from the imposition of meaning. Behind this proclamation one discerns a deeper understanding: he is referring to the evils linguistic differences encourage. Rather abstractly, Schwitters explains:

> Abstract poetry evaluates values against values. You could also say "words against words." This makes no sense, but it creates the

sense of a world, and that is what matters. (The common soldier must show respect and deference to every officer.)

Transference of the artist's worldview. (Callus and corn ointment in a society at peace, war merchandise.) Total experience greens brain, but the shaping is what matters.... And you? (Sign up for war bonds!) Decide for yourself what is poem, what is frame.

The dada movement, back in 1916, had proclaimed that government lies led to World War I. Literary historian Jed Rasula explains, "[Hugo] Ball, like so many other artists, flinched at the platitudes used to whip up martial fever, he felt that language itself was being poisoned." Kurt Schwitters' response, after the war, had been to take scraps of these poisoned languages and reassemble them into collage, concocting fresh language with no denotation—no corrupt social meaning.

Schwitters said, "The *Ursonate* is the most purely abstract of my poems." All instrumental music is abstract: music without lyrics makes no referential statement. When language is similarly freed from making referential statements—as with *Ur Sonata*—our unconscious can freely apprehend.

Abstract words seem funny; we laugh. Then, as the poem begins to sound beautiful, we feel joy. Credit Kurt Schwitters with awakening the joyous, preverbal awareness we experienced as little kids.

Consider the schoolbook series from the sixties, *Phonics Is Fun.* Is it fun learning to read? Through phonics lessons, beginning readers figure out that phonemes are meaningless letter-combinations lodged inside of words: "-at" is in cat and hat. The picture of a cat wearing a hat is funny. But Kurt Schwitters is funnier than phonics, immersing us in a phonemic bath that never dries up into meaning. His *Ur Sonata* theme *tatta tatta* frees "-at" of any mission to denote cat or hat. In *Ur Sonata,* phonemes escape social language; they attain the autonomy of musical notes— as in composer Oliver Nelson's song-title, "The Blues and the Abstract Truth." The abstract truth we experience bathing in Schwitters' sound poetry is transcendental. For an hour, we're transported to translingual Utopia.

In January 1937, Kurt Schwitters—that tall, blue-eyed, blond-haired man—fled for his life from Germany. The deadly serious Adolf Hitler and his propaganda minister Joseph Goebbels had singled out Schwitters as an exemplary degenerate artist, since in his collage-making Schwitters famously specialized in elevating garbage to the status of art-material. In June

1937, Hitler was photographed for a newspaper, standing in front of Kurt Schwitters' signature artwork, the *Merzbild* collage, confiscated from a museum and now hung, askew, in the "Complete Insanity" room of the "Degenerate Art" exhibition in Munich. In the photo, Hitler is laughing.

Score one for Schwitters, self-titled "bourgeois and idiot": he cracked up Hitler.

LIVING UR SONATA

I first heard *Ur Sonata* when I was a boy in the sixties—recited by my father. In the eighties, when I was performing it regularly, my audiences seemed to experience *Ur Sonata* as a novel discovery, not the landmark classic I knew it to be. Today—forty years on—an Internet search turns up dozens of *Ur Sonata* performances on *Youtube*, along with hundreds of articles and blogposts, yet few people I chat with in my bookstore are familiar with this century-old artwork.

Kurt Schwitters knew *Ur Sonata* could be a baffling poem, but he hoped it would outlive his era. His 1927 essay *Meine Sonate in Urlauten* aims to help make the poem accessible. The essay is descriptive ("The sonata consists of four movements...."), explanatory ("The gathering of the themes and inspirations was dadaistic and arbitrary...."), analytical ("Many interpretations are possible...imagination is required to read correctly...."), defensive ("Work improves the reader's receptivity much more than questions or thoughtless criticism...."), instructional ("Every performer can put together his or her own Cadenza based on the themes...."), and reflexive ("My explanations are a document concerning the inexplicability of a work of art, or, as Raoul Hausmann, puts it: 'First comes art, then piano playing.'").

In *Living Ur Sonata*—written a century after Schwitters—I too aim to help make the poem accessible. My tactic is to mix personal storytelling with historical narrative. *Ur Sonata* is a poem that's accompanied me for sixty years, offering joy and solace. I hope *Living Ur Sonata* assists you, dear reader, in gaining as much benefit as I have from Kurt Schwitters' delightfully baffling, profound composition.

Here are two reasons to celebrate Kurt Schwitters today especially: he puts us in touch with our common humanity, and he inspires us to defy our own era's resurgent nationalism. A hundred years after he composed it, let's conjure Kurt Schwitters to transcend authority and seize the hour, by singing *Ur Sonata*.

LIVING UR SONATA

PART ONE: TRANSCENDENCE

CHAPTER ZÄTT—THEMES 6, 12, 13, 14, 17

Schwitters survives…as one of the most extraordinary performers of the century. When he [recited] his *Primeval Sonata*—a long poem made up entirely of wordless sounds—it was as if there had come into existence a completely new mode of human expression, by turns hilarious and terrifying, elemental and precisely engineered. Others dreamed of reconciling art and language, music and speech, the living room and the cathedral, the stage and the unspoiled forest. Schwitters had the sweep of mind not only to dream of these things, but to carry them out.

—John Russell, *An Alternative Art*, 1974

October 10th, 2009
Main Street Park Gazebo
Easthampton, Massachusetts

"Priimittii, Priimiititti, Priimiititti too, Priimiititti taa," intones performance-poet and graphic journalist Rebecca Migdal, swinging her hair, swaying in her black-and-red Renaissance-fair gown.

Bailey, the toy poodle at our feet, growls.

Two cops who've pushed through the audience wave their arms.

"Priimiititti too, Priimiititti taa, Priimiititti tootaa, Priimiititti tootaa," Rebecca insists. Eric Blitz's ad-hoc punk percussion and DJ Glove's guitar/tape-measure mash-up are demanding answers. Holyoke community organizer Pronoblem Baalberith's PVC-pipe bass bubbles. Noise musician Bob Wilson's toy-store keyboard jangles. Expressionist painter Denis Luzuriaga's aloe-plant-operated synthesizers coo and belch. Hand-typeset printer Mitch Ahern's homemade electroluxopipophone roars to life—then gives up its ghost.

Bailey is howling.

"Wrap it up," one cop commands.

I lean my silver flute into the mic and expel a burst of free jazz. Priestess-of-Artemis Rebecca intensifies, "Priimiititti tuutaa, Priimiititti tuutaa, Priimiititti tootaatuu, Priimiititti tootaatuu."

The second cop runs his hand across his throat. Rebecca responds, "Priimiititti tuutaatoo, Priimiititti tuutaatoo."

Scrap-metal sculptor John Landino, who specializes in bolting books shut, abandons tuba, trumpet, and French horn, navigates our ten-member ensemble's maze of amps, and crosses to greet the cops. "You officers comfortable? Something to drink?"

Rebecca declaims, "Tatta tatta tuutaa too, Tatta tatta tuutaa too." Eric bangs his soup-pot. My flute punctuates the rising cacophony. Rebecca chants, "Tatta tatta tuiiEe tuiiEe, Tatta tatta tuiiEe tuiiEe. Tatta tatta tuiiEe tuiiEe, Tatta tatta tuiiEe tuiiEe." Barking with vigor, Bailey strains his leash.

Landino catches my eye. "Andy, how much longer?"

Rebecca is ranting, "Tilla lalla tilla lalla, Tilla lalla tilla lalla." Our troupe—Urchestra—is midway through the Cadenza, so, five minutes of this. The Finale will be three. I flash my fingers: we need five plus five minutes.

"Tilla lalla tilla lalla, Tilla lalla tilla lalla!"

"No," shouts the first cop. "It's after seven, you're in violation. Stop!"

Pronoblem—a Yeti in green beast-helmet and brown-fur gown—crosses to join Landino's negotiation. Temporary distraction.

Rebecca goes operatic, "Tuii tuii tuii tuii, Tuii tuii tuii tuii, Tee tee tee tee, Tee tee tee tee." I add my baritone; we duet, "Tuii tuii tuii tuii, Tuii tuii tuii tuii." I drop down as Rebecca glides up, "Tee tee tee tee, Tee tee tee tee. Tatta tatta tuiiEe tuiiEe, Tatta tatta tuiiEe tuiiEe." Guitar, cymbals and electroluxopipophone amp discordantly. "Tatta tatta tuiiEe tuiiEe, Tatta tatta tuiiEe tuiiEe."

Landino is winding his finger: pick it up. I gesture behind me, asking the group to cut volume. Into her mic, Rebecca whispers, "Tilla loola luula loola, Tilla luula loola luula, Tilla loola luula loola, Tilla luula loola luula."

DJ Glove's tape-measure screeches against his guitar.

I cough along, "Tuii tuii tuii tuii, Tuii tuii tuii tuii, Tee tee tee tee, Tee tee tee tee, Tuii tuii tuii tuii, Tuii tuii tuii tuii, Tee tee tee tee, Tee tee tee tee."

The second cop yells, "Stop!"

Eric's snare rolls.

I shout, "Ooo bee!"

DJ Glove's tape measure snaps.

Rebecca echoes, "Ooo bee!"

Mitch's electroluxopipophone roars.

I warn, "Ooo bee!"

Bailey howls. Eric bashes. Rebecca wonders, "Ooo bee?"

Bob flutters his keys. I double down, "Ooo bee!"

DJ Glove revs his electric sander. Rebecca moans, "Ooo bee."

Bailey on hind legs, barks, barks, and barks.

I relent, "Ooo bee."

Denis' synth is rising. Rebecca cheers, "Ooo bee!"

We raise arms for silence, gesturing for the audience to join, altogether now, with, "Ooooooooooooooooooooooooooooooooo."

I call over to the cops, "Two minutes."

They've calmed down. They're not Nazis.

CHAPTER ÜPSIILON

Nazi SA raided the office of Paul Renner, director of Munich's Master School for German Printers, on March 25th, 1933, seizing Renner's copy of Kurt Schwitters' literary journal, *Merz 24*—typeset and printed there the year before by typographer Jan Tschichold and his students. Under Hitler, only heavily-ligatured Germanic blackletter fonts like Fraktur were permitted. New typography—promoted by Jan Tschichold (author of *Die Neue Typographie*), along with Paul Renner and Kurt Schwitters—was an internationalist, form-follows-function practice condemned by Nazi chief propagandist Joseph Goebbels as *Kulturbolschewismus*: communism's advance-guard.

The SA was far too late to prevent distribution of *Merz 24*'s thousand copies. The issue's content was Schwitters' thirty-page *Ur Sonata*. Schwitters had developed this sound-poem through iteration and reiteration, between 1921 and 1932, during dozens of scandalous performances at avant-garde theater evenings, private parties and fancy salons throughout Europe. He'd published excerpts previously, for instance, in Eugene Jolas' Paris quarterly *transition*, and Arthur Lehning's Dutch *i 10* arts review.

After the March 1933 raid, Paul Renner was fired from his college directorship, and the font he'd created, Futura (this font you're now reading), was banned. Jan Tschichold was imprisoned for a month, then escaped to Switzerland and England, where he was hired by the founder of Penguin Books, Allen Lane, to design the standard Penguin paperback. Kurt Schwitters was dismissed from his bread-and-butter position as chief graphic designer to the city council of his hometown, Hannover, and the Nazis began to include his typographically adventurous books and magazines in public book-burnings.

The Nazis had already been exhibiting Schwitters' controversial collages of garbage-scraps in their touring *Entartete Kunst* ("Degenerate Art") shows. Since the nineteen-twenties, according to biographer Gwendolen Webster, "[Schwitters'] works, and by extension his own person, [had been] branded as repulsive, schizophrenic, seditious, and an insult to the whole country." Now in the nineteen-thirties, *Neues Volk* magazine called Schwitters' art,

> Simply indescribable trash... That the *Merzbild* could even be purchased from public city funds testifies more to the business sense than to the artistic talent of [its] creator.

Schwitters did not stop touring. Harriet Janis, co-founder of the Sidney Janis Gallery in Manhattan, recounts Walter Spengemann's tale that,

> He began enlivening his poetry lectures with a most dangerous kind of audience participation. Opening that strange, omnipresent, cabalistic portmanteau of his, he would remove a photograph of Hitler and place it at the platform's edge. Before launching into the long *Ursonate*...he would invite his audience to spit at Hitler's likeness whenever they felt so inclined. This, he implied, would be an acceptable substitute for applause.

CHAPTER IKS—THEMES 1, 6

March 18th, 2010
MUCCC (Multi-Use Community Cultural Center)
Rochester, New York

"I must take responsibility for what you hear tonight," my cheery, rumpled father, retired behavioral toxicology professor Victor Laties, tells an audience composed mostly of old high-school musician friends, along with our beloved, rebellious jazz-band director, Ned Corman.

"In 1949," Dad explains, "I was studying German in college, and I read a nonsense poem called *Priimiittitti,* in an anthology of writing from *transition,* the nineteen-twenties European literary journal. Years later, I used to recite *Priimiittitti* to my children: Nancy, Andy, and Claire. They grew up, and Andy learned there was more to *Priimiittitti.* He started performing the long version of *Priimiittitti* as a jazz piece. Tonight, his jazz-band friends Mitch, Don, and

Steve—happy fiftieth birthday, Steve—with new friends Rebecca and Eric, will perform *Priimiittitti* for you. So, I hope you can forgive me."

Broadway-musical preparator Don Rice's three saxophones and twenty heirloom bells are arrayed next to songwriter/bandleader Steve Rice's accordion and keyboard. Multi-Use Community Cultural Center is their brother Doug Rice's place.

Eric Blitz's percussion paraphernalia are deployed upstage, near Mitch Ahern's assortment of homemade instruments. Rebecca Migdal, a pirate queen in flowing headdress, and I, two saxes jostling my chest, take center stage.

Steve's piano rumbles. Eric's cymbals rustle. Don's bells ping, his soprano sax burbles. Rebecca and I announce, "Fümmmmmmmmmmms!"—she ascending, me descending. Steve's piano rises with us, until, together, Rebecca and I land on, "Bö wö tää zää Uuuuuuuu," me gliding up this time, while she goes silent.

Eric's cymbals are jangling. Turning to me, Rebecca squawks, "Pögiff!"

Rim-shot from Eric. Mitch's crutch-synth squeals. I try calm Rebecca with, "Kwiee—eeeeeee." Don's tenor sax offers tuneful subtones.

We reconcile, with "Ooooooooooooooooooooo."

After the show, Ned Corman congratulates us: "You ripped it up."

CHAPTER WEE

I felt liberated and wanted to exclaim my joy to the world. I was thrifty and used whatever I could find…. You can also shout using garbage, and that's what I did, by gluing and nailing it together. I called this Merz. It was my prayer to celebrate the victorious end of the war; for once again peace had triumphed. Everything was broken anyway, so the task was to build something new from the shards. I painted, nailed, glued, wrote poems…. My *Anna Blume* triumphed, people despised me, sent me threatening letters, and avoided me.

—Kurt Schwitters, "Facts from My Life."

Transformations.

In 1921 Germany, Kurt Schwitters was already notorious for pasting posters of his nonsensically irreverent love-poem, "*An Anna Blume*" ("Blue is the color of thy yellow hair….") onto public-announcement street-columns. Next stop, Czechoslovakia. While rehearsing for their Prague performance—*Anti-Dada*—in Hannah Höch's Berlin apartment, Schwitters showed Höch and Raoul Hausmann the piece "*Alphabet von Hinten*" ("Alphabet in Reverse"): Z through A, except for J. Hausmann said it was "the first step to a sound poem," and pulled out a copy of one of his 1918 *Plakatgedichte* ("Poster Poems"): graphic found-art composed entirely of large letters, "fmsbwtözäu, pggiv-..? mü"—originally a print-shop type sample.

During the threesome's Prague show, Hausmann performed the fmsbwtözäu letters. On the trip home Schwitters obsessively vocalized the strange sequence. "He did not stop all day...it became a bit much," Hausmann later wrote.

At initial public recitals of the poem he later named *Ur Sonata,* Schwitters called it "Portrait of Raoul Hausmann."

Decades after, in 1946, from exile in the English Lake District, Schwitters reached out to Hausmann by mail; the two collaborated on a poetry journal called *PIN,* for "Poetry Intervenes Now" and "Presence Is New." The effort was cut short by Schwitters' illness, but *Kurt Schwitters and Raoul Hausmann and the Story of PIN* was published in 1962 by two Polish émigrés Schwitters had met in London, filmmakers Franciszka and Stefan Themerson, later the founders of Gaberbocchus Press. The *PIN* book's promo copy read, "TWO FAMOUS DADAISTS OF THE

'TWENTIES WROTE THIS BOOK IN THE 'FORTIES gaberbocchus PUBLISHES IT IN THE 'SIXTIES and hopes IT WILL BE READ IN THE 'EIGHTIES." The Gaberbocchus *PIN* was edited by the Themersons' niece, Jasia Reichardt.

The Beatles' album *Sgt. Pepper's Lonely Hearts Club Band* came out in 1967, featuring a collaged album-cover created by English pop artist Peter Blake, who had discovered collage fifteen years earlier, when he was in art school. Blake's roommate Richard Smith had been dating Jasia Reichardt, a Kindertransport refugee taken in by relatives. Reichardt described collages created by her Uncle Stefan and Aunt Franciszka Themerson's friend Kurt Schwitters. Smith told Blake; they began making collages.

Schwitters to Beatles.

The Beatles' 1968 "White Album" cover was designed by pop artist Richard Hamilton, who had already played a critical role in Schwitters' history. Hamilton in 1965 had organized the partial salvage of Schwitters' third *Merzbau*, an English Lake District sculptural installation known as the Elterwater Merz Barn.

While assistant professor of art at Newcastle University, Hamilton had recruited students to extract the wall-mounted portion of this deteriorating assemblage from inside its stonework barn.

Hamilton's team had packed the *Merzbau* wall onto a truck, transported it one-hundred-twenty miles from the village of Elterwater, and installed it into Hatton Gallery at Newcastle University.

Hamilton's "White Album" design included, packed within its austere blank jacket, a Schwitters-like poster collaging Beatles photos and memorabilia.

Schwitters to Beatles, again.

Like Peter Blake and Richard Hamilton, many young artists of the fifties who were seeking an alternative to the dominant Abstract Expressionist style took inspiration from Kurt Schwitters' abstract yet topical collages and absurdly humorous yet pointed poems and performances. Among Schwitters' American proponents was Fluxus co-founder Dick Higgins—whose innovative coinage "intermedia" well described Schwitters' discipline-busting practice (Higgins was father-in-law to Urchestra's DJ Glove, AKA Joshua Selman). In the newsletter of his Something Else Press, Higgins explained Schwitters' appeal to the new generation:

> Shoes serve and wear out. From the moment they are put on the feet, they are always changing, until the time when their change makes them less serviceable, irreversibly so, and they are discarded.

So many of the artists became unhappy about [the] eternal, unyielding quality in their art, and they began to wish their work were more like shoes, more temporary, more human, more able to admit of the possibility of change. The fixed-finished work began to be supplemented by the idea of a work as a process, constantly becoming something else, tentative, allowing more than one interpretation. We see it in literature in the controlled ambiguities of Joyce, William Carlos Williams, Abraham Lincoln Gillespie, Kurt Schwitters.

Another American admirer was *Monty Python's Flying Circus* collage-animator Terry Gilliam, and he wasn't the only Schwitters-lover among the Pythons. In *Monty Python's* very first episode, "Whither Canada"—broadcast October 5th, 1969—John Cleese plays a sports announcer breathlessly narrating a modern-artists' bicycle race, colleague Michael Palin at his side.

Pepperpot (*Michael Palin*): That's not Picasso—that's Kandinsky.

Sam Trench (*John Cleese*): Good lord, you're right. It's Kandinsky. Wassily Kandinsky, and who's this here with him? It's Braque. Georges Braque, the cubist, painting a bird in flight over a cornfield and going very fast down the hill towards Kingston and—Piet Mondrian—just behind, Piet Mondrian the neoplasticist, and then a gap, then the main bunch, here they come, Chagall, Max Ernst, Miro, Dufy, Ben Nicholson, Jackson Pollock, and Bernard Buffet making a break on the outside here, Brancusi's going with him, so's de Chirico, Fernand Leger, Delaunay, De Kooning, Kokoschka's dropping back here by the look of it, and so's Paul Klee dropping back a bit and, right at the back of this group, our very own Kurt Schwitters.

Pepperpot: He's German!

But Cleese's claim was understandable: Schwitters wasn't just a proto-Python, his application for British citizenship had finally been approved days before his death. On January 8th, 1948—with his English companion Wantee (Edith Thomas) by his side—Schwitters would have died an Englishman, if only he had emerged from his coma to sign the paperwork.

CHAPTER FAU—THEME 18

November 10th, 1984
Chicago Filmmakers

"Zätt üpsiilon iks, Wee fau Uu, Tee äss ärr kuu," moans performance-artist Lynn Book—Time Arts instructor at the School of the Art Institute of Chicago. Percussionist Johnse Holt thumbs his mbira; trumpet-player Jeff Beer squeezes a muted sigh.

"Pee Oo änn ämm, Ell kaa li haa," Lynn urges. "Gee äff Ee dee zee beee?"

Cellist Philip Hart Helzer has been bowing a drone. Now he leans to his mic, wondering if, "Zätt üpsiilon iks, Wee fau Uu, Tee äss ärr kuu." Johnse is shaking a rattle; Jeff's trumpet punctuates the letters. Phil plucks a dramatic cello chord, operatically adding, "Pee Oo änn ämm, Ell kaa li haa." Johnse strikes a conga, Jeff hums a buzz through his horn. Phil fears, "Gee äff Ee dee zee beee?"

Now it's my turn to sing the alphabet in reverse, except for J—and I end triumphantly on "Aaaaa."

Finally, Lynn, Phil and I conclude *Ur Sonata* with a fourth, simultaneous alphabetic recitation. But we get—painfully—only as far as "beeee?"

A hundred-odd audience members applaud. A robust elderly gentleman bursts forward to shake our hands. "I am Doctor Hansjuergen Kienast. My friend in New York for many years was Richard Huelsenbeck."

How amazing to meet a living connection to dada!

Doctor Kienast has much to say. He'd loved our show. Huelsenbeck would have been so pleased that dada has a home in Chicago. How had we come to perform a German poem?

I am thrilled to be talking to this delightful man. But—something nags me. I do not bring it up, never in my subsequent letters to Doctor Kienast. Still—is he unaware of Richard Huelsenbeck's frequently critical attitude toward Kurt Schwitters?

Huelsenbeck was a communist participant in the 1918 German Revolution at the end of World War I, and he called Schwitters petty bourgeois. Schwitters responded to this attack from the political left in writing, positing two kinds of dada. Political dadas were "husk"—*huelse*—but pure dadas like Raoul

Hausmann, Hans Arp, and Tristan Tzara, were "core."

Kurt Schwitters declared allegiance to neither husk nor core dada. Instead, he was Merz, a one-man apolitical art movement. But for Schwitters, art and politics simply occupied different dimensions, and in a decade when the right-wing nationalist "stab-in-the-back" theory blamed Germany's World War I loss on Social Democrats and international Jewish conspiracy, Schwitters' supranational practice of border-transcending artistic collaboration showed clearly which side he was on. In 1925, he wrote,

> Nations exist, unfortunately. Nations cause wars. National art serves to reinforce a sense of union between people who call themselves a nation. National art paves the way for wars.... But ultimately, people exist independent of nations.... The highest task of art is to educate and to cultivate, for it expresses the feeling for humanity shared by the most noble people—at least sometimes.

Schwitters may not have set out, in the nineteen-twenties, to inject explicit politics into art, but his art certainly had political impact. As Stefan Themerson explained to friends in the Gaberbocchus Common Room, in 1958,

To us, today, it may perhaps seem that the act of putting two innocent words together, the act of saying:

"Blue is the colour of thy yellow hair,"

is an innocent aesthetic affair—that the act of putting together two or three innocent objects, such as a railway ticket, and a flower, and a bit of wood—is an innocent aesthetic affair. Well, it is not so at all. Tickets belong to railway companies; flowers to gardeners; bits of wood to timber merchants. If you mix these things together you are making havoc of the classification system on which the regime is established, you are carrying people's minds away from the customary modes of thought, and people's customary modes of thought are the very foundation of Order, whether it is the Old Order or the New Order, and, therefore, if you meddle with the customary modes of thought then, whether you are Galileo or Giordano Bruno with their funny ideas about motion, or Einstein with his funny ideas about space and time, or Russell with his funny ideas about syllogisms, or Schönberg with his funny ideas about the black and white keys of the keyboard, or the Cubists with their funny ideas about shapes, or Dadaists or Merzists with their funny ideas about introducing "symmetries and rhythms instead of principles"—you are, whether you want it or not, in the very bowels of political changes. Hitler knew it. And that is why Kurt Schwitters was kicked out of Germany. "Nothing is resisted with such savagery as a new form in art," writes Kandinsky, quoting a historian of the Russian theatre, Nelidoff.

In the nineteen-thirties, Kurt's teen son Ernst joined the Socialist Workers' Youth, smuggling information about the Nazis for publication abroad. Shortly afterward, Kurt and Helma Schwitters formally took a stand, becoming supporters of the left-liberal Social Democratic Party.

CHAPTER UU

Collective Unconscious: Hermes, Mercury, Merz.

Schwitters identified so fully with his one-man movement that he often signed letters "Kurt Merz Schwitters," and sometimes simply "Merz."

His word Merz—snipped with scissors from an advertisement and pasted into the collage later titled *Merzbild* ("Merz picture")—was in original context a middle syllable of *KOMMERZ UND PRIVAT BANK*. The German word *Kommerz*—from the Latin *com* + *mercari* (together + trade)—refers to Mercury, the Greek Hermes—God of commerce, tricksters, thieves and travelers, inventor of the lyre (gifted to Apollo in apology for stealing cattle), and psychopomp who escorts souls to the underworld.

At no time did Schwitters write anything about a Hermes/Mercury/Merz relation.

Kurt Schwitters was born June 20th, 1887: astrological sign Gemini, ruling planet Mercury.

Schwitters wrote, "I don't believe that...the time of birth...can tell anything about a person." ... "Seek your good fortune within; there you will find it."

But, says legendary philosopher-priest Hermes Trismegistus in the ancient text *Hermetica*, "As above, so below." Thus, planet Mercury magically influences cinnabar: vermilion-red mercury-sulfide crystal, the chemically-wedded "Philosopher's Stone"—in Arabic, *zinjifrah*, or "dragon's blood," in German, *zinnober*. Since antiquity, Spanish-mined cinnabar has been distilled to release metallic mercury: quicksilver.

Kurt Schwitters always used cinnabar-red paint for his trademark "KS" signature on collages and paintings.

The German word *zinnober* has a second definition: nonsense. My father was a toxicologist who in the nineteen-sixties helped prove that mercury—used historically in medicine and industry—is a heavy-metal poison that accumulates in the body, eventually causing tremors, speech disorders, and hallucinations. The phrase "Mad as a hatter"—as in the nonsensical Mad Hatter of Lewis Carroll's *Alice in Wonderland*—refers to the weirdness of nineteenth century hatmakers; this was due to toxic mercury nitrate used in felt. By the twenty-first century, mercury was widely banned; few artists today would risk neuropathology just to paint in authentic red cinnabar.

Mercury to Merz: in 1928, archetypically mercurial Kurt Schwitters cofounded Hannover *Zinnoberfest,* a nonsense festival. In *Kurt Schwitters, A Portrait from Life,* frequent collaborator Kate Steinitz, recalls,

All the artists of Hannover forgot their "isms" and manifestos. Even the old-fashioned academicians became suddenly gay and made quite jolly drawings for the big event....

[Kurt Schwitters] turned up the idea of Cinnabar as the festival theme.... Naturally he wrote the text for the festival songs.... It was supposed to be the wildest, reddest Cinnabar ever held in red-decorated rooms! The songs came jumping full-fledged out of Kurt's head, just as Pallas Athena jumped out of the Greek god's.... "Jump right into the Cinnabar! Wallow in it!" ... [Concert pianist] Walter Gieseking composed the theme song...he let off steam in jazz, without inhibition....

Kurt Schwitters ducked in and out of the crowd when he wasn't dancing. He danced with powerful enthusiasm, even the very latest dances, all the while emitting his enraptured, "Arrr...." He really held his girls tight. It looked as if he might crack their ribs.

In 2000, Hannover's artists, gallery owners, and municipal cultural office honored Kurt Schwitters by resurrecting *Zinnober;* they now present the arts festival every fall. This way to the Cinnabar!

CHAPTER TEE

June 26th, 2009
Holyoke, Massachusetts

"Vegan cupcake?" calls James Bickford to a passing car. The driver stops, his window opens, an arm extends. James moves close with a tray of green cakes. A selection process, a taste test, and the gratified driver inquires, "Say, what's going on here?" Canal-side, twenty neighbors sit at folding tables, chatting over paper plates and plastic cups filled with free food and drink. Behind them, eight more tables groan under the platters of goodies provided by all.

It's Bring Your Own Restaurant (BYOR), the open-to-anyone gatherings Bickford invented a few months ago. If the police are aware of these pop-up potlucks—which take place on public roadsides—

they've decided not to get entangled. Social Democrat James Bickford—also known as Pronoblem—is good at attracting media attention.

Eric Blitz and I have just arrived from Manhattan: I'd left the bookstore I run in Amherst, at Eric Carle Museum of Picture Book Art, just past two, picked up Eric and his equipment on 28th Street before five, and gotten back to Paper City Studios at seven—in time for dinner at BYOR. By eight, we're up on the third floor in Rebecca Migdal's Gonzo Comix loft, finishing with the set-up of Eric's percussion.

It's time again for Final Fridays, the community open mic Rebecca and I launched last January. A dozen poets and musicians will offer their work to neighbors and one another. The evening is structured around *Ur Sonata*, presented in three twenty-minute segments—interspersed with open mic guests. Anyone may join with *Ur Sonata*. Over the past months, ten performers have added themselves to the shifting ensemble we call Urchestra.

Our group is leaderless, with no direction for the improvisers. The only constraint is, each time, we declaim the entire *Ur Sonata*. This isn't about sounding good for listeners, but rather the direct experience of each artist in collaborative interaction with other artists and participating audiences.

Consider: encountering this thirty-page nonsense poem, we feel compelled to respond, since it's strange. If we reject, this is a missed chance. When we look at a Schwitters collage, on the wall of a museum, we can't hammer on our own stuff. In contrast, *Ur Sonata* invites us to become its next development. So, the most fruitful response is to declaim it our own way.

Performing *Ur Sonata* means joining Schwitters in his mystic zone.

The BYOR diners have drifted up into Rebecca's studio for Final Friday. The open mic's first *Ur Sonata* movement is ready to go. At the last minute, John Landino, Eric Blitz and I sneak down a side hallway to share a joint, in honor of Valerie Caris Blitz.

Valerie can't be here this time, though she accompanied Eric from Manhattan for our March show, when she participated by creating an action-painting to our sound-art. She came also in May, bringing a roll of twenty huge, rapidly-completed, abstract paintings. We'd pinned these up, completely covering a wall of Rebecca's studio, and then—as a thunderstorm raged outside the window-wall overlooking Holyoke Canal—in front of Valerie's paintings, we'd played *Ur Sonata.*

Valerie is an important member: she presented *Ur Sonata* in 1984 Berlin with performance artist Wolfgang Müller's group *Die Tödliche Doris* ("The Deadly Doris"). But Valerie's been in hospital for weeks. She'd finally had enough of how her AIDS cocktail made her feel, and she went off her meds. A few days after our May *Ur Sonata*, a mouth infection turned to pneumonia. She's in St. Vincent's—the AIDS hospital on Twelfth Street—unconscious.

We've had a few puffs, Landino has offered an invocation to Valerie, and we're moving down the hall toward Rebecca's studio.

The landlord is in our way. "Were you smoking weed? The cops could shut my building down!"

I'm stoned, sensing Valerie possibly on her deathbed. "I'm sorry. I didn't think—"

I never realized how huge he is. He leans, growls, "You didn't think; you smoked. You had to smoke your ma-ri-jua-na. In my building."

I expect he will back away. He does not. He gets close to our faces, repeating, "You want-ed to smoke your MA-RI-JUA-NA."

Eric has slipped off. Landino tries, "Hey, brother—"

"I'm talking to Andy."

"I'm sorry. I apologize. We won't do it again. Please. We've got a house."

He steps aside.

As we move toward the studio, filled with friends and neighbors, Landino murmurs, "I think I just lost my mojo."

CHAPTER ÄSS

Schwitters' work, and the magical exaltation of the object, give the first hint of the place of modern art in the history of the human mind, and of its symbolic significance. They reveal the tradition that was being unconsciously perpetuated. It is the tradition of the hermetic Christian brotherhoods of the Middle Ages, and of the alchemists, who conferred even on matter, the stuff of the earth, the dignity of their religious contemplation.

—Aniela Jaffé and Carl Jung, *Man and His Symbols*

Nonsense, abstract, nonrepresentational: these labels define by negation. Why be negative? To protect the status of sense, rationality, and representation.

As nonsense performance-poets and abstract artists, we seek—and strive to provide access to—higher dimensions of experience. So, best to call *Ur Sonata* not nonsensical, but transcendent. Best to call Kurt Schwitters' and Valerie Caris Blitz's collage and painting not abstract, but visionary. Hermes, Mercury, Merz.

Kurt Schwitters had a one-man show in 1944 London, at Jack Bilbo's Modern Art Gallery. Art historian Herbert Read—theorist of anarchism and, later, editor-in-chief of the English translation of *Collected Works of C.G. Jung*—wrote in his introduction to the Schwitters exhibition catalog,

> An art of *abstract incantation*…to hear Schwitters recite his poems is to be convinced that he has invented still another art form….
>
> I doubt if Schwitters would like to be called a mystic, but there is nevertheless in his whole attitude to art a deep protest against the chromium-plated conception of modernism. The bourgeois loves slickness and polish: Schwitters hates them. He leaves his edges rough, his surfaces uneven. He realizes that the created object is always an approximation to the imaginative conception, and that it is only the

fussy and irrelevant intellect that would like to give precision to the organic reality of art.

Schwitters was so pleased with Read's essay that he included copies in correspondence with galleries and patrons in America.

CHAPTER ÄRR—THEMES 11, 15, 16

August 12th, 1989
Emit Gallery

Lynn Book is a working performance artist, creating original pieces and presenting around the country. Once a year, she phones me with an *Ur Sonata* opportunity.

School of the Art Institute of Chicago students have gotten hold of an abandoned warehouse in the West Loop, for one night only. They call it Emit Gallery. They've lighted the space with a dozen gigantic candles suspended from wood beams. Each candle has six flaming wicks. This gallery of shadows is jammed with a hundred art students. Lynn has also invited a dozen kids from her neighborhood; they sit up front.

Last summer, I bought ten-foot-long, one-foot-wide industrial hoses which we cut, assembled, and wore as costumes for our ten shows at Harry Hoch's place on Elston, Cabaret Voltaire. We're wearing our crazy hose-outfits now.

Lynn and I thrive on participation: we get people revved up in the Presto, chanting rhythmically, "Grimm glimm gnimm bimbimm, Grimm glimm gnimm bimbimm, Grimm glimm gnimm bimbimm, Grimm glimm gnimm bimbimm, Grimm glimm gnimm bimbimm, Grimm glimm gnimm bimbimm, Grimm glimm gnimm bimbimm, Grimm glimm gnimm bimbimm." During the *Durcharbeitung,* when I'm haranguing like a politician—"Graaaaa graaaaa, Graaaaa graaaaa," and "EkeEke ekeEke ekeEke ekeEke, EkeEke ekeEke ekeEke ekeEke, EkeEke ekeEke Rrrumm! EkeEke ekeEke Rrrumm! EkeEke ekeEke Rrum, Rrum! EkeEke ekeEke Rrum, Rrum! Rrum Rrum Rrum Rrum, Rrum Rrum Rrum, Rrum!"—Lynn is in the audience shouting back, while distributing pieces of gardenhose and handfuls of black-eyed peas. People are spitting peas at me through the hose-peashooters.

The kids go nuts. They're marching, shouting *Ur Sonata,* spitting peas.

Dada is supposed to be provocative. Everyone knows this, so, no-one at a dada show can be provoked. But some of these college students don't like the kids' unruliness and start walking out.

Most of the crowd stays with us, yelling along. Mid-cacophony, I find myself extending hose-encased arms upward and complaining, *"Eli, Eli, lama sabachtani?"* No one hears.

Transcendental.

CHAPTER KUU

"If that's art, I'm a Hottentot," declared President and racist-in-chief Harry Truman. Further, "I don't pretend to be an artist or a judge of art, but I am of the opinion that so-called modern art is merely the vaporings of half-baked lazy people."

The year was 1947. Highly publicized congressional hearings had condemned the US State Department's *Advancing American Art,* as a waste of taxpayer funds. This huge exhibition—pushing anticommunist PR about free expression in capitalist America—had been touring to international acclaim since 1946. Now it would be recalled, its hundred-and-seventeen paintings sold off cheap.

Simultaneous with this anti-modern-art grandstanding by conservative US politicians, Kurt Schwitters, over in the English Lake District, successfully solicited three thousand dollars from the Kaufmann Family—modern-art-loving Pittsburgh department-store magnates. Now Schwitters was awaiting the money's disbursal by his financial intermediary, the Museum of Modern Art (MOMA), in New York.

Art historian Adrian Sudhalter delicately explains,

> The issue was entrusted to the museum's legal counsel and drawn out for many months.... The complexities of postwar international law delayed the delivery of the fellowship to Schwitters for over a year.... Schwitters proposed constructing a...*Merzbau* in England, and of using part of the scholarship to underwrite a recording of his *Ursonate*, the second of his two life works.... Sadly, Schwitters only received the first two payments of his fellowship, in increments of $250, before his death in January 1948. Two more payments in the same amount were used to underwrite his burial.

"Used to underwrite his burial." Schwitters meets Kafka.

But really: what made MOMA sit on Schwitters' money for a year, when he was living in poverty and could not afford medical treatment?

What "postwar international law" prevented rapid disbursal of US funds to an artist living in ally England who'd personally corresponded with his US patrons?

Let's be honest. MOMA was paranoid word would leak they'd sent funds to a crazy German abstract artist overseas, giving an opening to the *New York Post* and right-wing politicians.

Two years later, the Central Intelligence Agency was the secret founder of Congress for Cultural Freedom. CCF toured Abstract Expressionist exhibitions internationally, resuming the propaganda war contrasting America's "free enterprise painting" with the Soviet Union's state-mandated representational style, Socialist Realism.

The CIA didn't seek authorization to found CCF: they already knew their political bosses despised abstract art. According to Porter McCray, who in 1953 became director of the (also secretly CIA-funded) MOMA International Program,

> This was the context in which [founding MOMA curator] Alfred Barr felt compelled to write a scathing article in a 1952 issue of the *New York Times Magazine* titled, "Is Modern Art Communistic?," which compared statements about modern art made by Eisenhower, Truman, and Churchill to those made in Nazi Germany and the Soviet Union.

CHAPTER PEE—THEME 5

I myself deployed Schwitters' abstract art to bridge cultures, on behalf of anticommunist free enterprise. From "Trading Places"—chapter six of my memoir, *Rebel Bookseller*:

> In January of '95, American Booksellers Association education director Willard Dickerson called me up and asked me to sit down. "Andy, how would you like to be dean of this fall's booksellers school in Latvia?"
>
> The Children's Bookstore was headed into a demanding year. Since October of '94 we'd been running a small full-time outlet at Chicago Children's Museum's location on North Pier. Now we were immersed in planning the museum's much larger shop at Navy Pier, to be opened in September of '95. We also had

seventy-five book fairs on the docket. The count of superstores in the Chicago area had risen to eighteen, six of them close to us.

But how could I say no? I'd taught at several ABA schools, and I loved them.

ABA's Eastern European program had been going for several years—it was a function of the Soros Foundation's Open Society Institute. OSI had identified bookstores as some of the threatened institutions to try to assist in their transition from the centralized economic system of the communist era to the free-for-all capitalist marketplace now emerging, since bookstores perform a vital informational and educational function in every free society. I'd been on the American Booksellers Association education committee when this overseas schools program had launched, and I'd alerted Willard I'd like to get involved.

* * *

After the first day of their September booksellers school, the forty Latvian booksellers are visibly uneasy. We've been told one of the difficulties is tension dating from the period when they'd been locked together into the Soviet bookselling bureaucracy. Some of the booksellers had done cruel things to others. Now they are trying to run their shops like independent competitive capitalist enterprises. It isn't easy for them to relax and act collegial.

At dinner I announce there will be a special lecture and everyone should assemble back at the hall at 8 PM. No one is happy about this but they do all come. My colleagues—Stan Bolotin of Harvard Book Store, Tracy Danz of Zondervan Publishers, and Valerie Lewis of Hicklebee's Children's Books—present storytelling performances and songs before my lecture, so the Latvian booksellers are alert something unusual might be coming.

I step to the podium, clear my throat, and launch into *Ur Sonata*. After a minute—as I'm emotionally declaiming, "Dll rrrrr beeeee bö, Dll rrrrr beeeee bö fümms bö, Rrrrrr beeeee bö fümms bö wö, Beeeee bö fümms bö wö tää, bö fümms bö wö tää zää, fümms bö wö tää zää Uu," but Berutha is providing no translation—the booksellers begin to express annoyance.

Berutha interrupts me, "Is it German poetry? From the early twentieth century? Is it Christian Morgenstern?"

I'm delighted. Morgenstern was a nonsense poet who preceded Schwitters by a decade; I love *"Das Grosse Lalula"* and Morgenstern's other *Gallows Songs*. I tell Berutha it's Kurt Schwitters' classic *Ur*

Sonata. She gives the booksellers a quick explanation. She has a degree in poetry!

I continue with *Ur Sonata* and realize something is happening I've never experienced in my decade performing with Lynn Book. Our audiences were English speakers, so the text was always non-English, but here, the syllables are equally non-English and non-Latvian. Although our day of bookselling classes has been spent communicating via translator, now we need no translation. *Ur Sonata* blossoms translingual.

Valerie, Tracy, and Stan coach the group to join in chanting. We transform to a jolly ensemble.

CHAPTER OO—THEME 4

August 6th, 2009
Lower East Side

"Rr rr rr rr rr rr rr rr rr rr rum!" drawls Bowery Poetry Club founder Bob Holman.

Rebecca Migdal tries placating with, "Rrummpff tillff toooo? Ziiuu ennze ziiuu nnzkrrmüüü, ziiuu ennze ziiuu rinnzkrrmüüüü!"

Unsatisfied, Bob demands, "Rr rr rr rr rr rr rr rr rr rr rr rr rum!!!"

Rebecca urges, "Rrummpff tillff toooo? Ziiuu ennze ziiuu nnzkrrmüüü, ziiuu ennze ziiuu rinnzkrrmüüüü!"

I side-comment, "Rakete bee bee!"

Bob is fanatical, insisting, "Rr rr rr rr rr rr, Rr rr rr rr rr rr, Rr rr rr rr rr rr, Rr rr rr rr rr rrumm!!!!!!"

Rebecca strives with him, "Rrummpff tillff toooo? Ziiuu ennze ziiuu nnzkrrmüüü, ziiuu ennze ziiuu rinnzkrrmüüüü!"

I have to point out, "Rakete bee bee."

Bob—exhausted—relents: "Rakete bee zee."

An emotional evening, this cremation-expense fundraiser for Valerie Caris Blitz, who passed away last week. Onstage, our ten regular Urchestra players are joined by comix artist Fly on guitar, and punk rocker Steve Wishnia on double bass. Among our dozens of friends—batting around black balloons I placed under every chair—are Fluxus co-founder Alison Knowles, who performed Schwitters in the sixties, and Lower East Side counterculture historian Clayton Patterson. Bob Holman has contributed the venue and—himself a longtime *Ur Sonata* performer—joined the show. His cowboy accent is a stimulating twist. Finishing the Cadenza, Bob slips, cutting himself on his wine glass. He concludes our backwards alphabetization freely bleeding, a martyr to poetry.

CHAPTER ÄNN

I cannot agree that I should pray. I cannot see
any point as God has different concerns.
—Kurt Schwitters, Letter to Helma, 1940

Behind his family's cottage, fourteen-year-old Kurt
Schwitters created a garden with roses, strawberries,
an artificial mountain, and a reconstructed pond.
Bullies destroyed the private paradise. Poor Kurt had
an hours-long attack he later called St. Vitus Dance—
really an epileptic seizure.

More seizures—sometimes several daily—kept Kurt
isolated. He graduated high school at twenty.
Although he suffered attacks in adulthood, they were
less frequent: he learned to stave off seizures with
physical activity—walking and bicycling in town,

hiking in the mountains, dancing at parties—plus an assortment of pharmaceuticals.

In 1920, Schwitters wrote of his teen years,

> My interests changed because of the illness. I discovered my love for art. Initially, I composed rhyming couplets in the manner of music-hall comedians. During a full moon one autumn night I noticed the clear, cold moon. From then on, I composed poetry in a lyrical, sentimental manner. Then music seemed to me to be *the* art. I learned to read music and played music all afternoon. In 1906 I saw my first moonlit landscape in Isernhagen and began to paint. One hundred watercolor landscapes by moonlight, painted from nature. Lit by stearin candles. I decided to become a painter.

Martyrdom redeemed by creativity. Of Schwitters' collage work, art historian Jonathan Fineberg asks,

> Could his detachment with regard to his materials and his project of reorganizing fragmentary experience have been a symbolic reordering informed at least in part, by his epilepsy?

The Nazis listed epilepsy as a condition to be eradicated. A critical task for Schwitters became to avoid seizing in public, since this could bring arrest, concentration camp and death. Before the Nazis though, Schwitters was already exploring themes of martyrdom. His 1919 story *Die Zwiebel* ("The Onion") tells of a king ordering the narrator's gruesome execution and evisceration. The king then eats our narrator's eyeballs; this causes the king's horrible death. The narrator's body is reassembling, he's resurrected! The princess begs him to bring back the king, too. Narrator instead blows up the king.

In 1940, Schwitters was imprisoned, along with thousands of other refugees, at Hutchinson Internment Camp on the Isle of Man: the English had decided any German might be a spy. The leading lights of German liberal culture, penned together, created a university for themselves, giving lectures and running discussion groups. Kurt helped launch a series of performance evenings, regularly reciting *Ur Sonata* and his other poems.

Outward sociability as a survival technique, concealing inward distress. In autumn 1940 letters from internment camp to Helma, Kurt wrote,

> I go to our church, unable to believe in the love of humankind.

Still, at the deepest level, he retained faith:

> I retreat more and more from the rules of the Church, but I am still religious....
>
> At night I hold conversations and you appear to answer. In spite of war and separation we belong to each other, forever and all eternity.

PART TWO: REMEMBRANCE

CHAPTER ÄMM—THEME 1

In recent years, both Eberhard Blum, a German flutist connected with SUNY-Buffalo, and Peter Froehlich of the English Theatre at the University of Ottawa, have performed this poem brilliantly, each of them surpassing Schwitters' own partial recording.
—Richard Kostelanetz,
Text-Sound Texts, 1980

March 8th, 1979
Yale University

"Tesch, Haisch, Tschiiaa; Haisch, Tschiiaa." I'm in the last pew. Passing Dwight Chapel after class, I'd noticed the sign. Schwitters—from dad's *Priimiittitti*—free, now?!

"Haisch, Happaisch; Happapeppaisch." The dark-suited actor radiates energy as he recites a piece he'd called "Fury of Sneezing." Forty people are up close, I'm alone back here. "Happapeppaisch; Happapeppaisch; Happapeppaisch; Happa peppe; TSCHAA!" These abstract sound-poems—absurd dialogues—non-sequitur vignettes: seriously funny.

Ten-minute break. He's back, announcing, dramatically, *Die Sonate in Urlauten*. Takes his time. Deep breath. And.... "Fümms bö wö tää zää Uu, pögiff, kwii Ee, Oooooooooooooooooooooo." His command, possession, force of will! And there's so much! Beautiful in a way I've never experienced. Unpredictable, yet familiar and—romantic. Backwards alphabets? So moving.

I'm producer for Yale Dramat Children's Theater Company—we've got Lewis Carroll's nonsense poem *The Hunting of the Snark* touring schools now. I'm always looking for pieces to adapt. This Schwitters poem? Half hour: the right length.

Too weird for schools. Leaving church, I read on the sign: Peter Froehlich.

* * *

Midnight, May 5ᵗʰ, 1979
Yale University

"Bö, bö, bö, bö, bö, böwö, böwö, böwö, böwö, böwö, böwö, böwörö, böwörö, böwörö, böwörö, böwörö, böwörö, böwöböpö, böwöböpö, böwöböpö, böwöböpö, böwöböpö, böwöböpö, böwöröböpö, böwöröböpö, böwöröböpö, böwöröböpö, böwöröböpö, böwöröböpö...."

After four hours of thirty sound-poems recited by shifting clusters of Sheep's Clothing's fifteen members, Scott M. is reading *Ur Sonata*.

If I hadn't seen Peter Froehlich's one-man show eight weeks ago, I'd be thinking Scott was doing great just to pronounce the syllables. But I know how wonderful this piece can be. Scott's version is monotonous, relentless, unending. I want to leave.

How would I stage *Ur Sonata*?

CHAPTER ELL—THEMES 8, 9, 10

DADA, DADA, URSONATA!
Ecstatic nonsense is every child's birthright! All ages will gurgle and coo over Kurt Schwitters' 1920's Dada masterwork, *Ursonata* (Primeval Sonata), performed for children by Lynn Book and Andy Laties. Two Saturdays: Sept. 12th & 19th, 10:30 AM. Please reserve ahead. Free.
—Press release, The Children's Bookstore, 1992

"Lanke trr gll, pe pe pe pe pe, Ooka ooka ooka ooka," sings Lynn Book. We're costumed in our industrial hoses. I respond, "Lanke trr gll, Pii pii pii pii pii, Züüka züüka züüka züüka."

She's wiggling fingers at the dozen babies in the front row, proposing, "Lanke trr gll, Rrmmp, Rrnnf."

I query, "Lanke trr gll, Ziiuu lenn trll? Lümpff tumpff trll."

She assures me, "Lanke trr gll, Rrumpff tilff too."

Not satisfied, I check, "Lanke trr gll, Ziiuu lenn trll? Lümpff tumpff trll."

She reminds me that, "Lanke trr gll, pe pe pe pe pe, Ooka ooka ooka ooka."

I recall also that, "Lanke trr gll, Pii pii pii pii pii, Züüka züüka züüka züüka."

She's wiggling fingers at the babies, "Lanke trr gll, Rrmmp, Rrnnf."

I agree, "Lanke trr gll."

Why did I wait all these years to perform *Ur Sonata* for kids? Over a hundred people attend these performances, among them my own children, Sam and Sarah, aged five and three. Everyone—baby, grade-schooler, parent—ooo-ooo-ing, grimm-glimming, tilla-lalla-ing along.

It makes sense. Ernst Schwitters wrote:

> I shall never forget those many "MERZ-evenings," where, as a four-, five-, and six-year-old, I used to have my regular place in the centre of the front row of seats, directly opposite my father, marveling open-mouthed at him.
>
> It was during those evenings that the Sonata grew. It never was read off a manuscript, although in its various stages of development it had been published in art-magazines

everywhere. But my father knew it by heart, and preferred to improvise the recital, as this gave him the chance to develop it continuously. Thus a great many people became witnesses of the slow development of this unique piece of—shall we say—"music" and/or abstract poetry.

Of course, Ernst's presence informed Kurt's experience and shaped his performance. *Ur Sonata* had to be perfect for children.

64

CHAPTER KAA—THEME 1

He yelled, he sniffled, he barked; his *rrr* rolled;
his body, his hands vibrated with the rhythm of
his words, flabbergasting, hypnotizing his
audience.

    —Kate Steinitz, *Kurt Schwitters: A Portrait
from Life*

Noon, September 4th, 2010
Dada Invasion of West Haven
West Haven Beach, Connecticut

Psych-med interaction, seizure, ambulance fuck-up.

The first seizure is the most dangerous. Sam will
not have a second.

He was twenty-three.

It's two weeks later.

People look unreal. I've started wearing sunglasses.

Rebecca is in Seattle for niece Chani's wedding. Bailey and I have driven the hour-and-a-half from Holyoke. We're strolling from the van to the bandstand, where Landino in white gown, Bob Wilson, Pronoblem in grass-covered camo coverall, Steve Lindow, Denis Luzuriaga, and DJ Glove are testing mics and plugging together gear.

Pulling on his leash—Bailey has seen a squirrel.

Landino calls over, "You okay, Andy?"

"I'm fine."

He comes off the stage and hugs me. "Four months," he says. "You'll be okay in four months."

"I don't know about it," I manage.

What a terrible thought, that I should ever get over losing the person I loved more than anyone in the world.

I'm sitting at a picnic table. Bob Wilson joins me, offering, "My friend was twenty-five when he killed himself. Schizophrenia. His mom gave me his guitar."

I smile. "That's great she did that."

Wow, people do not know what to say to me.

The group is warming up onstage, but I can't do that. I crouch on the ground, blowing trumpet-blasts through my gardenhose. Bailey barks and howls. Landino bends down a mic. I share it with Bailey.

It's time to start. I climb onto the bandstand, tying Bailey's leash near my feet.

Performance-poet Stephen Lindow is standing in for Rebecca. A few days ago, we ran through the text. He doesn't particularly know *Ur Sonata,* but he's a great vocal improvisor. Depending on how I hold up, he may find himself carrying the show.

Guitar, synths, and tuba build a bed of sound. I'm glad to be adding a few saxophone notes. Last week, my old roommate Tobias wrote me a Facebook message: "Play a sax solo for Sam." I will when I can.

I glance at Steve; we lean into our mics.

Slow, forceful, melodic: "Fümms bö wö tää zää Uu, pögiff, kwii Ee; Oooooooooooooooooooooo." We're off.

We're swimming.

He's enjoying this, so—me too: I'm in tune with his enthusiasm. I'm suddenly all *Ur Sonata,* bouncing familiar dialogic syllables back and forth.

"Fö."

"Bö."

"Fö."

"Bö."

"Fö."

"Bö."

"Fö."

"Bö."

"Fö."

"Bö."

"Fö."

Bailey has been growling; now he yips and jumps.

"Böwö."

"Fümmsbö."

"Böwö."

"Fümmsbö."

"Böwö."

"Fümmsbö."

"Böwö."

"Fümmsbö."

"Böwö."

"Fümmsbö."

"Böwörö."

Bailey's got a pattern: bark twice, wait, bark twice, wait, bark twice. Thrice!

"Fümmsböwö."

"Böwörö."

"Fümmsböwö."

"Böwörö."

"Fümmsböwö."

"Böwörö."

"Fümmsböwö."

"Böwörö."

"Fümmsböwö."

"Böwörö."

"Fümmsböwö."

Bailey's now barking in erratic clusters. On hind legs, he strains his muzzle up—barking, barking.

"Fümmsböwötää."

"Böwörötää."

"Fümmsböwötää."

"Böwörötää."

"Fümmsböwötää."

"Böwörötää."

"Fümmsböwötää."

Bailey's now mixing bark-clusters with jumping and howling.

Steve and I have been voicing this as a quarrelsome conversation, but we've switched to flirtation.

"BöwörötääzääUu pö."

"FümmsböwötääzääUu pö."

"BöwörötääzääUu pö."

"FümmsböwötääzääUu pö."

"BöwörötääzääUu pö."

"FümmsböwötääzääUu pö."

"BöwörötääzääUu pö."

"FümmsböwötääzääUu pö."

Howling, howling, howling, Bailey, firmly seated, howls, howls, howls.

"BöwörötääzääUu pö."

"FümmsböwötääzääUu pö."

"BöwörötääzääUu pö."

"FümmsböwötääzääUu pö."

Steve and I blame each other for ruining the love, but—we desperately need to make up.

"BöwörötääzääUu pögiff."

"FümmsböwötääzääUu pögiff."

"BöwörötääzääUu pögiff."

"FümmsböwötääzääUu pögiff."

"BöwörötääzääUu pögiff."

"FümmsböwötääzääUu pögiff."

"BöwörötääzääUu pögiff."

"FümmsböwötääzääUu pögiff."

"BöwörötääzääUu pögiff."

"FümmsböwötääzääUu pögiff."

True confessions:

"BöwörötääzääUu pögiff

"FümmsböwötääzääUu pögiff."

Silence.

Bailey yips. We forgive:

"Kwiiee."

"Kwiiee."

"Kwiiee."

"Kwiiee."

"Kwiiee."

"Kwiiee."

"Kwiiee."

"Kwiiee."

"Kwiiee."

"Kwiiee."

"Kwiiee."

"Kwiiee."

Bailey is prone.

CHAPTER II—THEME 3

I heard Schwitters practising his *Lautsonate* in the crown of an old pine on the beach at Wyk on Föhr. He hissed, swished, chirped, fluted, cooed and spelled.
    —Hans Arp

April 18th, 2011
Bushwick, Brooklyn

"Zikete bee bee, Rinnzekete bee bee, Rakete bee bee," I demonstrate, tapping my foot.

I'm in a bedside chair. Jenny Gonzalez, sitting on the bed, joins the jazzy rhythm, chanting "Zikete bee bee ennze, Rinnzekete bee bee ennze, Rakete bee bee ennze." Eric Blitz taps on the desk while we sing. Jenny warns, "Don't annoy Bonney and Luna!" Too late, their two rats are nosing the bars.

In a few days, we'll drive up to MUCCC, in Rochester, for a return gig.

Eric and Jenny have been together for a year—she's seen several Urchestra shows; now she'll join the group. Jenny's a painter, singer, performance-poet, and contributor of comix to *World War 3 Illustrated,* the long-running political-comix magazine where Rebecca Migdal is an editor, and for which Eric and I provide musical accompaniment during slideshow performances.

"Schwitters didn't perform it this way," I tell Jenny. "At least—no one knows for sure how he handled it. His son Ernst made a recording in 1958 that he said was the same way as his dad. But Ernst does it slow and unaccented—I don't believe Kurt was boring."

Eric asks, "Isn't Ernst the one who went around suing everybody?"

"He threatened Jaap Blonk and sued Eberhard Blum," I confirm. "They both had to withdraw their records. It wasn't just about rights: Ernst said you had to perform like Kurt. So, should John Coltrane play "My Favorite Things" like Julie Andrews?"

Jenny adds, "Or *Frankenstein* movies be like the book? Have you heard other versions of *Ur Sonata?*"

"Sure—lots are online, all different. It's crazy Kurt was never filmed."

Eric mentions, "We caught Kurt on Youtube."

"Right, you can hear the short part they recorded."

Jenny asks, "So, the way you've been doing it–?"

"Just how I started in the eighties—with jazz rhythms. How I heard it. But you should totally do it how you hear. It would be great if you'd do it differently. Steve Lindow did it his own way, last September."

Eric remarks, "We need to issue a record. We keep talking about it, but we don't do anything. It's as much my fault as anyone's."

"Yeah, Pronoblem is sitting on all those recordings he's made—he must have a dozen on his computer. We should edit together the best parts. I guess none of us has time."

LIVING UR SONATA

CHAPTER HAA

Kurt Schwitters wanted to preserve his ever-evolving *Ur Sonata* for posterity, but it wasn't clear how to accomplish this. Ernst Schwitters writes:

> Kurt Schwitters had realized all along, that a phonetic way of noting down the *Sonate* was essential, if it should not die with him... With each successive publication he improved on the form of notation, and finally, in 1932, the *Sonate in Urlauten* was published as his last number of the *MERZ* magazine, no. 24. But although this is undoubtedly the most phonetic way of notation to date, it is virtually impossible to recite it correctly, simply by reading it. A prime necessity is, that one has heard Kurt Schwitters recite it as often as possible.

Audio documentation was the obvious solution. In 1924, Kurt Schwitters edited together a three-minute recording, featuring selections from a dozen phonetic themes. Biographer Gwendolen Webster suggests,

> Recipients of the *Merz* magazine…must…have been taken aback to find that *Merz* 13 was a gramophone record with Kurt reciting…from the *Ursonate*.

Creating the record had been a challenge. Art historian Kevin Concannon explains,

> Kurt Schwitters was among the first to approach sound recording as a plastic medium. Using sound film, Schwitters edited and collaged his nonsense poems after he recorded them and before he pressed them into records.

Preserving the relatively short sampler of themes had been a big project. To capture the entire piece, Schwitters would need professional help. But the second time he was able to record *Ur Sonata*—in 1932, at the studio of Southern German Broadcasting Company—time permitted, once again, only a thematic selection, featuring primarily the "Lanke trr gll" Scherzo.

As the years passed, uprooted by flight from Nazis, Schwitters continued to seek an *Ur Sonata* recording opportunity. Exiled, in 1947, weakened by heart disease and a stroke, Kurt finally got his chance. Outrageously, because of middle-brow *BBC* taste, the recording was not to be. Gallery owner E.L.T. Mesens explains that his place,

> London Gallery organized two MERZ Poetry Recitals. Their reception by the public was characteristic of the post-war mind. If I say that there was a total lack of interest, I am not exaggerating! At the first reading, Wednesday, 5th March, 1947, the attendance was of sixteen people including two journalists.

Stefan Themerson was also there:

> Two gentlemen from the *BBC* were invited and came. The idea was that they would record the *Ur Sonata*. Just record it. Schwitters read his *Ur Sonata,* but the gentlemen left in the middle.

Kurt Schwitters referred to *Ur Sonata* as the second of his two masterpieces. His principal lifework had been his Hannover "Cathedral of Erotic

Misery"—later called *Merzbau*—an elaborate complex of constructions developed continually over fifteen years, occupying first his art studio and subsequently more and more of his house's interior. During World War II, while Kurt lived as a refugee in London, his hometown of Hannover was playing a major industrial and logistical role in support of the German war effort. On the night of October 8th, 1943, five-hundred-and-four Royal Air Force bombers attacked military targets and residential neighborhoods in Hannover. Schwitters' house was hit, his *Merzbau* ruined—surviving now only in photos and the written recollections of its visitors.

When Schwitters died in 1948, the unique way he declaimed *Ur Sonata* had not been documented. Just as the Hannover *Merzbau* was lost, so Schwitters' masterful *Ur Sonata* performance also was lost.

CHAPTER GEE—THEME 7

Sent: April 25th, 2016
Subject: Ursonate performance for Bailey

Bailey has a mass in his throat—we can't afford the biopsy and MRI so we don't know if it's malignant, but he is on painkillers and steroids which seems to be enabling him to eat again. As for whether he would survive surgery and likely subsequent chemotherapy—at a cost of possibly $10,000—it's all too depressing to focus on. So—we thought of at least—a medical benefit concert in which he could perform as a member of his ensemble.

June 3rd, 2016
Spanish Harlem

"Aaaaaaaaaaaaaaaaaaaa," yells Jenny, encouraging the audience to cut loose. Eric's crashing cymbals heighten the energy.

I'm running Bank Street Bookstore in Manhattan now, and have the privilege to be playing Japanese shakuhachi-flute every few months with free-jazz legends Karl Berger and Ingrid Sertso, in the new incarnation of their forty-member Creative Improvisers Orchestra—first convened back in the seventies. Our CIO concerts are held in the *Casa de Musica* at El Taller Latino Americano, run by Rebecca's old friend Bernardo Palombo—who has provided his space to us for this Urchestra evening.

Rebecca calls, "Bee bee bee bee bee." DJ Glove's twanging guitar supports a blues run from Don Rice's soprano sax.

John Landino's not here: he's had esophageal cancer. It's in remission, but he can't travel.

As Eric's snare rolls, Jenny and the audience are yelling a lower note, "Aaaaaaaaaaaaaa."

Don on soprano and I—on alto sax—exchange sonic bursts, while Rebecca chants, "Zee zee zee zee zee."

Pronoblem's not here. His back and leg are bothering him. Cortisone injections only help so much.

Jenny and the group shout an even lower note, "Aaaaaaaaaaaaaaaa." DJ Glove's electric sander revs.

Rebecca intones, "Rinnzekete, bee, bee." Don and I sustain a long-tone chord.

Jenny and company hit a much lower note: "Aaaaaaaaaaaaaaaaa." Eric's cymbals shimmer.

Mournfully, Rebecca calls, "Enn ze, enn ze."

All together, in pain, we cry, "Aaaaaaaaaaaaaaaaaaaaaaaaaa," thinking of Bailey, howling in spirit.

Two weeks ago, we put him to sleep.

CHAPTER ÄFF

> I slept in a small glassed-in porch off the dining room. There was a huge chest near my couch; the first night I was astonished to hear distinct stirrings inside it. At breakfast I felt impelled to mention the phenomenon. The twelve-year-old Schwitters boy had filled it with guinea pigs.
> —Paul Bowles, *Without Stopping*

Kurt Schwitters had a special relationship with animals. Inside his Hannover house, this meant lots of pet guinea pigs.

On January 2nd, 1937, Kurt left for Norway—secretly. He'd learned the SS was planning to interview him about the political activities of his friends; Helma's mother was pro-Nazi and if she'd known Kurt was fleeing, she might warn the SS. Ernst was already in Lysaker, outside Oslo. Helma remained in Hannover to safeguard the house full of Kurt's art and to look after her father, her Nazi mother, Kurt's mother Henriette, and the guinea pigs.

For three years, living with Ernst outside Oslo, Kurt kept up professional life, painting, making collages, writing letters, traveling, and assembling another *Merzbau*. But he spent part of every summer on the remote island of Hjertøya, where, based in a storage shed—the *Merzhytta*—he created in solitude. While he worked, Kurt habitually sang *Ur Sonata*.

In 1940, the Nazi invasion of Norway pushed northward. Kurt and Ernst engaged in a dangerous flight, during which Kurt used pet mice to manage stress, helping stave off an epileptic seizure (he did have a seizure later, after they'd crossed the North Sea to Scotland). Biographer Gwendolen Webster relates,

> An English soldier remembered how he was struck by the sight of a figure standing perfectly still during an air-raid alarm. While everyone else scrambled for shelter, the man merely took some white mice from a jacket pocket and let them loose. When the soldier found an opportunity to question him, the man replied: "Yes, I run after them and try to catch them. You see, I can't bear the torments and harassment of alarms anymore. I can't stand it!

So, I thought to myself that it would be better if I catch the mice. Then I don't hear the alarm, then I don't register the war, then I don't take any notice of aeroplanes, then I am not afraid and just concentrate on getting the little animals back again." When I asked him for his name, he replied, "I am Kurt Schwitters from Hannover."

Fifty-seven years later, on June 11th, 1997, during a pilgrimage to Schwitters' long-abandoned *Merzhytta* on Hjertøya, Wolfgang Müller—Valerie Caris Blitz's *Die Tödliche Doris* performance partner—was startled when,

All of a sudden, I heard a starling uttering strange sounds [...] Somehow these sounds had a familiar ring. Suddenly I realized that the bird was reciting parts of the *ursonate* which some unknown ancestor had picked up from Schwitters long ago and transmitted over generations. Starlings are known to be masters of imitation [...]. They learn the song from their parents (or parts of the song). Here, parts of the original *ursonate* had been transmitted without notice by the world of art.

CHAPTER EEE—THEME 2

March 1980
Uptown, Chicago

I've been living in Chicago for seven months, working as a receiving clerk for a B. Dalton Bookseller chainstore on North Michigan Avenue. I'm dating my boss.

I dropped out of Yale to study music with the Association for the Advancement of Creative Musicians. My once-a-month teacher is sax and flute master Douglas Ewart. I also take twice-weekly theater improv lessons with Josephine Forsberg, founder of Players Workshop of Second City. I rehearse every other night with singer/songwriter

Ellen Rosner's band, Fine Tuning. I perform in schools sometimes, as Jim Hawkins in *Treasure Island,* opposite Earth Theater founder Rudolf Munro's Long John Silver.

One night, I get home to find in my mailbox a thick nine by twelve manilla envelope from Germany. On the outside is the familiar handwriting of my high-school underground newspaper co-editor Laura Kelsey. I wait till I'm at the kitchen table in my eighth-floor studio apartment before opening the package.

Laura is spending her junior year in Munich. Her letter explains how, on receiving my request, she'd visited the university library, and yes, there were the collected works of Kurt Schwitters. Five volumes. She'd copied the pages I needed.

I flip the stack. So beautiful. I can hear Peter Froehlich.

I try reciting. It comes out jazz. Tapping my foot, I sing, off-beat, "Dedesnn nn rrrrr, li Ee, mpiff tillff toooo. Dedesnn nn rrrrr, desnn nn rrrrr, nn nn rrrrr, nn rrrrr, liiii Eeeee, m, mpe, mpff, mpiffte, mpiff till, mpiff tillff, mpiff tillff toooo. Dedesnn nn rrrrr, li Ee, mpiff tillff toooo, Dedesnn nn rrrrr, li Ee, mpiff tillff toooo tillll. Dedesnn nn rrrrr, li Ee, mpiff tillff toooo, tillll, Jüü-Kaa?"

Will I ever perform it?

***

March 1997
Downtown, Chicago

Lynn Book moved to New York a few years ago; last March, she had a solo *Ur Sonata* show in Brooklyn, at Roulette. I'm working a thousand hours a week at our new Navy Pier place: Children's Museum Store. A regular customer from my killed-by-chainstores Children's Bookstore mentions, at the register, that he saw a photo of me in the MCA.

What?

I make a guess and contact Lynn. A couple months ago, a Museum of Contemporary Art curator phoned, asking for relics of our *Ur Sonata* shows to include in the exhibit *Art in Chicago, 1945-1995*. Lynn dug up some photos and a piece of gardenhose.

I've got to see this. Our store is super-busy, but I zip over on a Sunday morning.

The museum is packed: I've never seen a crowd like this at the MCA. I'm scanning left and right: it's paintings, sculptures, more paintings. On the lower level, there's a Time Arts side-exhibit. There, in a plexiglass case, sits a five-inch segment of green hose, plus a photo of Lynn and me doing one of our Club Lower Links shows, wearing industrial hoses.

Thousands and thousands of Chicago artists—fifty years' worth—and from all these—along with the two-hundred-odd others in this retrospective—the curators chose us.

CHAPTER DEE—THEMES 3, 11

We play until death comes to fetch us.
—Kurt Schwitters, Letter to Christof
Spengemann, 1946

February 14th, 2017
Anchor House of Artists
Northampton, Massachusetts

Sparkling kaleidoscopic swirls, projected from *Youtube* onto our portable movie screen, morph, burst and implode. We've muted the robotic text-to-synth *Ur Sonata* soundtrack because nine Urchestra members provide live accompaniment for Pronoblem's abstract animation. It's our first time together since Bailey's memorial.

"Rakete rinnzekete, rakete rinnzekete, rakete rinnzekete, rakete rinnzekete, rakete rinnzekete, rakete rinnzekete," sing Rebecca and Jenny, as I riff on flute, before stopping to point out, "Beeeee bö."

Borrowed motorcycle, curving gravel road. Last September eleventh, Pronoblem died.

His son Miles is sitting in on guitar. John Landino's neighbor Jack Nelson contributes double bass, Landino himself is playing trumpet, Eric Blitz is on percussion, DJ Glove's on sander, tape-measure, and guitar. Bob Wilson brought homemade synths.

Psychopomps of Merz.

Today is Pronoblem's birthday, and the city of Holyoke has officially designated it James Bickford Day. Maybe some city councilors are privately glad Pronoblem isn't going to annoy them anymore—but at least they've honored his love for Holyoke.

We're stomping and shouting, "Bumm bimbimm, bamm bimbimm, Bumm bimbimm, bamm bimbimm, Bumm bimbimm, bamm bimbimm, Bumm bimbimm, bamm bimbimm, Bemm, bemm, Bemm, bemm, Bemm, bemm, Bemm, bemm."

For us to play, does one of us have to die?

CHAPTER ZEE—THEME 18

December 15th, 2017
Easton, Pennsylvania

"Zätt üpsiilon iks, Wee fau Uu, Tee äss ärr kuu," Rebecca, Jenny and I exclaim, as Eric crashes behind us. "Pee Oo änn ämm, Ell kaa li haa, Gee äff Ee dee zee beeee?"

We've taken advantage of our book-release tour supporting *Fight Fascism!*—the new issue of *World War 3 Illustrated* attacking Trump—to squeeze in an *Ur Sonata* evening at Book & Puppet Company, the place Rebecca and I just launched. Artist's-book maker Maryann Riker—one of our Mangled Myths puppet-show regulars—sits with a friend. Maryann asks, "Andy and Rebecca, have you met Lette?" We have not: we only moved to Easton this year, when I got fired by Bank Street College.

Turns out we're not the only dada refugees around here: eighty-two-year-old Lette Eisenhauer, the taboo-busting young Fluxus performance artist from the sixties, is one of our neighbors.

CHAPTER BEEEE?—THEME 1

October 5th, 2021
To: Eric Blitz

How is your recovery going? I have been thinking about our resolution back in 2010 that we would do an album together. Because I'm in Karl Berger's extended circle, I can use a studio up in Woodstock for low price. It's also possible through Karl's *Patreon* program to work with him.

When Pronoblem died, his hard drive of Urchestra music became inaccessible. Then, his *Fluxmass* Internet account went offline; links he'd posted to *Pennsound's* Kurt Schwitters webpage no longer worked. As the years passed—with Eric's health crises, my heart surgery, mom's and dad's deaths—to make a professional Urchestra recording was feeling more urgent.

* * *

August 8th, 2022
Clubhouse Studio
Rhinebeck, New York

"Fümms bö," whisper, mutter, and chant Jenny Gonzalez-Blitz, Rebecca Migdal, and Creative Music Studio co-founder Ingrid Sertso—born 1934 in Mannheim, Germany—overlapping, disjunct, simultaneous. "Fümms bö wö," they intone, garbling and tangling the syllables. "Fümms bö wö tääää?" It's chaos at their mics.

"Fümms bö, fümms bö wö, Fümms bö wö tää zää Uuuu?" They're the Three Fates, Clotho, Lachesis, and Atropos, conjuring and invoking, furious and ecstatic, spinning, measuring, and cutting the thread of life—Wantee, Helma, and Henriette, "Rattatata tattatata tattatata."

Creative Improvisers Orchestra director Karl Berger—born 1935 in Heidelberg—ranges up and down the grand piano, Eric's percussion percolating, my shakuhachi all hiss, swish, chirp, and coo.

February eighth, after surgery, John Landino passed away. Last Sunday, in Montague Center, Eric, Jenny, Mitch, Bob Wilson and I played John's memorial *Ur Sonata*.

"Rinnzekete bee bee nnz krr müüüü?" The voices collide, overlap, and merge.

"Fümms bö," they mourn. Karl's chords block and roll.

"Fümms böwö," they pray. Eric's cymbals tingle. My shakuhachi's unsure.

"Fümms bö wö täää?????"

PHOTOS

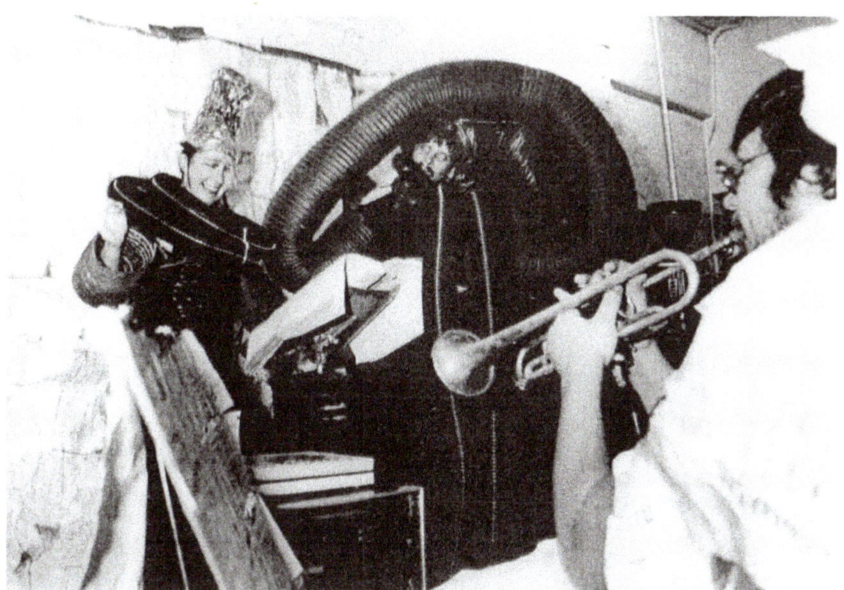

Lynn Book and Andy Laties wearing hoses, with Jeff Beer wrapped in *Ur Sonata* pages. Cabaret Voltaire, Chicago. 1988.

URSONATE URCHESTRA

Urchestra flyer designed by Rebecca Migdal. Top row, Eric Blitz, Rebecca Migdal, Andy Laties, and DJ Glove (Joshua Selman); bottom row, Mitch Ahern, Denis Luzuriaga, John Landino, and Pronoblem (James Bickford). Holyoke. 2009.

DJ Glove (Joshua Selman), Eric Blitz, Rebecca Migdal, John Landino, Andy Laties. Holyoke. April 2009.

Eric Blitz, percussion, in front of Valerie Caris Blitz paintings. Gonzo Comix Studio, Holyoke. June 2009.

Rebecca Migdal, DJ Glove, Bob Holman. Bowery Poetry Club, Manhattan. August 2009.

Steve Rice, Don Rice, Rebecca Migdal, Andy Laties, Mitch Ahern. MUCCC, Rochester. March 2010.

John Landino, Bailey the Poodle, Pronoblem (James Bickford), Andy Laties, Steve Lindow, Bob Wilson. Dada Invasion of West Haven. 2010.

"New York Scary Tale" by J. Gonzalez-Blitz. Pictured: Andy Laties, Jenny Gonzalez-Blitz, and Eric Blitz. Brooklyn. 2011.

Ingrid Sertso, Rebecca Migdal, and Jenny Gonzalez-Blitz. Clubhouse, Rhinebeck. 2022.

Ingrid Sertso, Rebecca Migdal, Karl Berger, Paul Antonell, Oliver Dog, Andy Laties, Eric Blitz, J. Gonzalez-Blitz. Rhinebeck. 2022.

Ur Sonata rehearsal: Bailey the Poodle, with Andy Laties on chromatic harmonica. Holyoke. 2009.

UR SONATA

by kurt schwitters

from Merz 24; facsimile reproduction

Ursonate

einleitung:

Fümms bö wö tää zää Uu,

         pögiff,

           kwii Ee.   **1**

Oooooooooooooooooooooooooooooooo,   **6**

  dll rrrrrr beeeee bö,   (A) **5**

  dll rrrrrr beeeee bö fümms bö,

    rrrrrr beeeee bö fümms bö wö,

      beeeee bö fümms bö wö tää,

        bö fümms bö wö tää zää,

        fümms bö wö tää zää Uu:

erster teil:

thema 1:

Fümms bö wö tää zää Uu,   **1**

         pögiff,

           kwii Ee.

thema 2:

Dedesnn nn rrrrrr,   **2**

      Ii Ee,

        mpiff tillff too,

          tillll,

         Jüü Kaa?

         (gesungen)

thema 3:

Rinnzekete bee bee nnz krr müü?   **3**

        ziiuu ennze, ziiuu rinnzkrrmüü,

  rakete bee bee.   **3a**

thema 4:

Rrummpff tillff toooo?   **4**

Ziiuu ennze ziiuu nnzkrrmüü,
Ziiuu ennze ziiuu rinnzkrrmüü,

   rakete bee bee? rakete bee zee.

Fümms bö wö tää zää Uu,
Uu zee tee wee bee fümms.

      rakete rinnzekete   (B)
      rakete rinnzekete
      rakete rinnzekete
      rakete rinnzekete
      rakete rinnzekete
      rakete rinnzekete
      Beeeee
      bö.

fö
     böwö
fümmsbö
     böwörö
fümmsböwö
     böwörötää
fümmsböwötää
     böwörötääzää
fümmsböwötääzää
     böwörötääzääUu
fümmsböwötääzääUu
     böwörötääzääUu pö
fümmsböwötääzääUu pö
     böwörötääzääUu pögö
fümmsböwötääzääUu pögö
     böwörötääzääUu pögiff

fümmsböwötääzääUu pögiff
    kwiiEe.

    rakete rinnzekete   (C) u3+
    rakete rinnzekete   3 a
    rakete rinnzekete
    rakete rinnzekete
    rakete rinnzekete
    rakete rinnzekete
    Beeeee
    bö.

fö
    böwö   1
fümmsbö
    böwörö
fümmsböwö
    böwöböpö
fümmsböböpö
    böwöröböpö
fümmsböwöböpö
    böwörötääböpö
fümmsböwötääböpö
    böwörötääzääböpö
fümmsböwötääzääböpö
    böwörötääzääUu böpö
fümmsböwötääzääUu böpö
    böwörötääzääUu pögö
fümmsböwötääzääUu pögö
    böwörötääzääUu pögiff
fümmsböwötääzääUu pögiff
    kwiiee.

    rakete rinnzekete   (D) u3+
    rakete rinnzekete   3 a

rakete rinnzekete
rakete rinnzekete
rakete rinnzekete
rakete rinnzekete
Beeeee
bö.

bö
bö
bö
bö
bö
böwö
böwö
böwö
böwö
böwö
böwö
böwörö
böwörö
böwörö
böwörö
böwörö
böwörö
böwöböpö
böwöböpö
böwöböpö
böwöböpö
böwöböpö
böwöböpö
böwöröböpö
böwöröböpö
böwöröböpö
böwöröböpö
böwöröböpö

böwöröböpö
böwörötääböpö
böwörötääböpö
böwörötääböpö
böwörötääböpö
böwörötääböpö
böwörötääböpö
böwörötääzääböpö
böwörötääzääböpö
böwörötääzääböpö
böwörötääzääböpö
böwörötääzääböpö
böwörötääzääböpö
böwörötääzääUu böpö
böwörötääzääUu böpö
böwörötääzääUu böpö
böwörötääzääUu böpö
böwörötääzääUu böpö
böwörötääzääUu böpö
böwörötääzääUu pögö
böwörötääzääUu pögö
böwörötääzääUu pögö
böwörötääzääUu pögö
böwörötääzääUu pögö
böwörötääzääUu pögö
böwörötääzääUu pögiff
böwörötääzääUu pögiff
böwörötääzääUu pögiff
böwörötääzääUu pögiff
böwörötääzääUu pögiff
böwörötääzääUu pögiff
fümmsböwötääzääUu pögiff
fümmsböwötääzääUu pögiff
fümmsböwötääzääUu pögiff

fümmsböwötääzääUu pögiff

fümmsböwötääzääUu pögiff

fümmes bö wö tää zää Uu,

pögiff,

kwiiee

kwiiee

kwiiee

kwiiee

kwiiee

kwiiee.

Dedesnn nn rrrrrr,   **(E)**   **2**

        Ii Ee,

            mpiff tilff toooo;

Dedesnn nn rrrrrr

  desnn nn rrrrrr

    nn nn rrrrrr

      nn rrrrrr

        Iiiii

         Eeeeee

           m

           mpe

           mpff

           mpiffte

           mpiff tilll

           mpiff tillff

           mpiff tillff toooo,

Dedesnn nn rrrrr, Ii Ee, mpiff tillff toooo,

Dedesnn nn rrrrr, Ii Ee, mpiff tillff toooo, tillll

Dedesnn nn rrrrr, Ii Ee, mpiff tillff toooo, tillll, Jüü-Kaa?

                                (gesungen).

Fümms bö wö tää zää Uu, pögiff, kwiiee.   **ü:**

Dedesnn nn rrrrrr, Ii Ee, mpiff tillff toooo, tillll, Jüü-Kaa.   **1**

                                (gesungen)   **2**

Rinnzekete bee bee nnz krr müüüü, ziiuu ennze ziiuu   **3**

          rinnzkrrmüüüü,
Rakete bee bee.

Zikete   bee bee   (F)   **3**
Rinnzekete bee bee
Rakete   bee bee
Zikete   bee bee ennze
Rinnzekete bee bee ennze
Rakete   bee bee ennze
Zikete   bee bee nnz krr
Rinnzekete bee bee nnz krr
Rakete   bee bee nnz krr
Zikete   bee bee nnz krr müüüü
Rinnzekete bee bee nnz krr müüüü
Rakete   bee bee nnz krr müüüü
Zikete   bee bee nnz krr müüüü, ziiuu
Rinnzekete bee bee nnz krr müüüü, ziiuu
Rakete   bee bee nnz krr müüüü, ziiuu
Zikete   bee bee nnz krr müüüü, ziiuu ennze
Rinnzekete bee bee nnz krr müüüü, ziiuu ennze
Rakete   bee bee nnz krr müüüü, ziiuu ennze
Zikete bee bee nnz krr müüüü, ziiuu ennze ziiuu rinnzkrrmüüüü
Rinnzekete bee bee nnz krr müüüü, ziiuu ennze ziiuu rinnzkrrmüüüü
Rakete bee bee nnz krr müüüü, ziiuu ennze ziiuu rinnzkrrmüüüü,
Rakete   bee bee.
Rummpfftillfftoooo?
Ziiuu ennze ziiuu nnz krr müüüü, ziiuu ennze ziiuu rinnzkrrmüüüü;
Rakete   bee bee,
Rakete   bee zee.

Fümms bö wö tää zää Uu, pögiff, kwiiee.   **U:** **1**
Dedesnn nn rrrrrr, Ii Ee, mpfiff tillff toooo, tillll, Jüü-Kaa.   **2**
                                          (gesungen)
Rinnzekete bee bee nnz krr müüüü, ziiuu ennze ziiuu   **3**
          rinnzkrrmüüüü,

Rakete bee bee.
Rrummpff tillff toooo?

Rum!   **(G)**
Rrummpff?
Rum!
Rrummpff t?
Rr rr rum!
Rrummpff tll?
Rr rr rr rr rum!
Rrummpff tillff?
Rr rr rr rr rr rum!
Rrumpff tillff toooo?
Rr rr rr rr rr rr rum!
Rrummpff tillff toooo? Ziiuu!
Rr rr rr rr rr rr rr rum!
Rrummpff tillff toooo? Ziiuu ennze!
Rr rr rr rr rr rr rr rr rum!
Rrummpff tillff toooo? Ziiuu ennze ziiuu!
Rr rr rr rr rr rr rr rr rr rum!
Rrummpff tillff toooo? Ziiuu ennze ziiuu nnzkrrmüüüü!
Rr rr rr rr rr rr rr rr rr rr rum!
Rrummpff tillff toooo? Ziiuu ennze ziiuu nnzkrrmüüüü,
   ziiuu ennze ziiuu rinnzkrrmüüüü!
Rr rr rr rr rr rr rr rr rr rr rr rum!!!
Rrummpff tillff toooo? Ziiuu ennze ziiuu nnzkrrmüüüü,
   ziiuu ennze ziiuu rinnzkrrmüüüü,
Rakete bee bee!
Rr rr rr rr rr rr
Rr rr rr rr rr rr
Rr rr rr rr rr rr
Rr rr rr rr rr rrumm!!!!!! *(gekreischt, mit erhobener stimme)*
Rrummpff tillff toooo? Ziiuu ennze ziiuu nnzkrrmüüüü,
   ziiuu ennze ziiuu rinnzkrrmüüüü,

Rakete bee bee,
Rakete bee zee.

Fümms bö wö tää zää Uu, pögiff, kwiiee.
Dedesnn nn rrrrrr, Ii Ee, mpfiff tillff toooo, tillll, Jüü-Kaa.

(gesungen)

Rinnzekete bee bee nnz krr müüüü, ziiuu ennze ziiuu
      rinnzkrrmüüüü,
Rakete bee bee.
Rrummpff tillff toooo?

Rum!
    RrRrRrummpff?
Rum!
    RrRrRrRrummpff t?
Rum!
    RrRrRrRrRrRrummpff tll?
Rum!
    RrRrRrRrRrRrRrummpff tillff toooo?
Rum!
    RrRrRrRrRrRrRrRrummpff tillff toooo ziiuu!
Rum!
    RrRrRrRrRrRrRrRrRrummpff tillff toooo ziiuu ennze!
Rum!
    RrRrRrRrRrRrRrRrRrRrRrummpff tillff toooo? Ziiuu ennze
        ziiuu nnzkrrmüüüü,
Rum!
    RrRrRrRrRrRrRrRrRrRrRrRrRrummpff tillff toooo? Ziiuu
        ennze ziiuuz nnzkrrmüüüü, ziiuu ennze ziiuu
        rinnzkrrmüüüü!
Rum!
    RrRrRrRrRrRrRrRrRrRrRrRrRrRr RrRrRrRrRrRrRrummpff tillff
    toooo?
        Ziiuu ennze ziiuu nnzkrrmüüüü?

Ziiuu ennze ziiuu rinnzkrrmüüüü!
Rakete bee bee.
Rrrrummmm!!!! *(gekreischt)*
RrRrRrRrRrRr
RrRrRrRrRrRr
RrRrRrRrRrRr
RrRrRrRrRrRr
Rrrrrrrrrrrummmmmmpfffff tillffff tooooooo?
Ziiiiuu ennze ziiiiuu nnzkrrmüüüü?
Ziiiiuu ennze ziiiiuu rinnzkrrmüüüü!
Rakete bee bee?
Rakete bee zee.

Rakete rinnzekete
Rakete rinnzekete
Rakete rinnzekete
Rakete rinnzekete
Rakete rinnzekete
Rakete rinnzekete
Beeeee
bö

fö
    bö
fö
    bö
fö
    bö
fö
    bö
fö
    bö
fö
    böwö
fümmsbö

        böwö
fümmsbö
        böwö
fümmsbö
        böwö
fümmsbö
        böwö
fümmsbö
        böwö
fümmsbö
        böwörö
fümmsböwö
        böwörö
fümmsböwö
        böwörö
fümmsböwö
        böwörö
fümmsböwö
        böwörö
fümmsböwö
        böwörötää
fümmsböwötää
        böwörötää
fümmsböwötää
        böwörötää
fümmsböwötää
        böwörötää
fümmsböwötää
        böwörötää
fümmsböwötää
        böwörötää
fümmsböwötää

                böwörötääzää
fümmsböwötääzää
                böwörötääzää
fümmsböwötääzää
                böwörötääzää
fümmsböwötääzää
                böwörötääzää
fümmsböwötääzää
                böwörötääzää
fümmsböwötääzää
                böwörötääzääUu
fümmsböwötääzääUu
                böwörötääzääUu
fümmsböwötääzääUu
                böwörötääzääUu
fümmsböwötääzääUu
                böwörötääzääUu
fümmsböwötääzääUu
                böwörötääzääUu
fümmsböwötääzääUu
                böwörötääzääUu pö
fümmsböwötääzääUu pö
                böwörötääzääUu pö
fümmsböwötääzääUu pö
                böwörötääzääUu pö
fümmsböwötääzääUu pö
                böwörötääzääUu pö
fümmsböwötääzääUu pö
                böwörötääzääUu pö
fümmsböwötääzääUu pö

böwörötääzääUu pö

fümmsböwötääzääUu pö

böwörötääzääUu pögö

fümmsböwötääzääUu pögö

böwörötääzääUu pögö

fümmsböwötääzääUu pögö

böwörötääzääUu pögö

fümmsböwötääzääUu pögö

böwörötääzääUu pögö

fümmsböwötääzääUu pögö

böwörötääzääUu pögö

fümmsböwötääzääUu pögö

böwörötääzääUu pögö

fümmsböwötääzääUu pögö

böwörötääzääUu pögiff

fümmsböwötääzääUu pögiff

böwörötääzääUu pögiff

fümmsböwötääzääUu pögiff

böwörötääzääUu pögiff

fümmsböwötääzääUu pögiff

böwörötääzääUu pögiff

fümmsböwötääzääUu pögiff

böwörötääzääUu pögiff

fümmsböwötääzääUu pögiff

kwiiee kwiiee

kwiiee kwiiee

kwiiee kwiiee

kwiiee kwiiee

kwiiee kwiiee

kwiiee kwiiee

Fümms bö wö tää zää Uu, pögiff, kwiiee.

Dedesnn nn rrrrrr, Ii Ee, mpiff tilff toooo? Till, Jüü-Kaa.

(gesungen)

Rinnzekete bee bee nnz krr müü? ziuu ennze ziuu rinnzkrrmüüüü;

Rakete bee bee.

Rummpff tillff toooo?

Ziiuu ennze ziiuu nnskrrmüüüü, ziiuu ennze ziiuu rinnzkrrmüüüü;

Rakete bee bee,

Rakete bee zee.

Fümmsbö wö tää zää Uu,

Uu zee tee wee bee

    zee tee wee bee

    zee tee wee bee

    zee tee wee bee

    zee tee wee bee

    zee tee wee bee Fümms.

schluss:

Fümms bö   fümms bö wö   fümmes bö wö tääää?

Fümms bö   fümms bö wö   fümms bö wö tää zää Uuuu?

Rattatata tattatata tattatata

Rinnzekete bee bee nnz krr müüüü?

Fümms bö

Fümms böwö

Fümmes bö wö täää???? *(gekreischt)*

zweiter teil:

largo

(gleichmäßig vorzutragen. takt genau ⁴/₄. jede folgende reihe ist um einen folgenden viertel ton tiefer zu sprechen, also muß entsprechend hoch begonnen werden)

Ooooooooooooooooooooooooooooooo *(leise)*   (J)   6

Bee bee bee bee bee - - - - - - - -

Ooooooooooooooooooooooooooooooo

Zee zee zee zee zee - - - - - - - -

Ooooooooooooooooooooooooooooooo

Rinnzekete - - - bee - - - bee - - -

Ooooooooooooooooooooooooooooooo

änn ze - - - - - - änn ze - - - - - -

Ooooooooooooooooooooooooooooooo

Aaaaaaaaaaaaaaaaaaaaaaaaaaaaaaaa *(laut)*   (K)   7

Bee bee bee bee bee - - - - - - - -

Aaaaaaaaaaaaaaaaaaaaaaaaaaaaaaaa

Zee zee zee zee zee - - - - - - - -

Aaaaaaaaaaaaaaaaaaaaaaaaaaaaaaaa

Rinnzekete - - - bee - - - bee - - -

Aaaaaaaaaaaaaaaaaaaaaaaaaaaaaaaa

Enn ze - - - - - - enn ze - - - - - -

Aaaaaaaaaaaaaaaaaaaaaaaaaaaaaaaa

Ooooooooooooooooooooooooooooooo *(leise)*   (L)   6

Bee bee bee bee bee - - - - - - - -

Ooooooooooooooooooooooooooooooo

Zee zee zee zee zee - - - - - - - -

Ooooooooooooooooooooooooooooooo

Rinnzekete - - - bee - - - bee - - -

Ooooooooooooooooooooooooooooooo

änn ze - - - - - - änn ze - - - - - -

Ooooooooooooooooooooooooooooooo

dritter teil:

scherzo
(die themen sind karakteristisch verschieden vorzutragen)

Lanke trr gll *(munter)*	(M)	III
pe pe pe pe pe		8
Ooka ooka ooka ooka		
Lanke trr gll		III
pii. pii pii pii pii		9
Züüka züüka züüka züüka		
Lanke trr gll		III
Rrmmp		4
Rrnnf		
Lanke trr gll		III
Ziiuu lenn trll?		3
Lümpff tümpff trll		10
Lanke trr gll		III
Rrumpff tilff too		4
Lanke trr gll		III
Ziiuu lenn trll?		3
Lümpff tümpff trll		10
Lanke trr gll		III
Pe pe pe pe pe		8
Ooka ooka ooka ooka		
Lanke trr gll		III
Pii pii pii pii pii		9
Züüka züüka züüka züüka		
Lanke trr gll		III
Rrmmp		4
Rrnnf		
Lanke trr gll		

trio *(äußerst langsam vorzutragen.)*

Ziiuu iiuu (N) 3
   ziiuu aauu
      ziiuu iiuu
         ziiuu Aaa

Ziiuu iiuu 3
   ziiuu aauu
      ziiuu iiuu
         ziiuu Ooo

Ziiuu iiuu 3
   ziiuu aauu
      ziiuu iiuu

scherzo III

Lanke trr gll *(munter)* (O) 8
   pe pe pe pe pe
      Ooka ooka ooka ooka

Lanke trr gll III
   Pii pii pii pii pii 9
      Züüka züüka züüka züüka

Lanke trr gll III
   Rrmmp 4
   Rrnnf

Lanke trr gll
   Ziiuu lenn trll? 3
   Lümpff tümpff trll 10

Lanke trr gll II
   Rrumpff tilff too 4

Lanke trr gll III
   Ziiuu lenn trll? 3
   Lümpff tümpff trll 10

Lanke trr gll
    pe pe pe pe pe
        Ooka ooka ooka ooka

III
8

Lanke trr gll
    Pii pii pii pii pii
        Züüka züüka züüka züüka

III
9

Lanke trr gll
    Rrmmp
    Rrnnf

III
4

Lanke trr gll

III

vierter teil:

presto
*(der vierte Teil ist streng taktmäßig, außer den in der durcharbeitung
eingeschobenen rezitationen)*

thema 11:   (P) 11
Grimm glimm gnimm bimbimm
Grimm glimm gnimm bimbimm
Grimm glimm gnimm bimbimm
Grimm glimm gnimm bimbimm
Grimm glimm gnimm bimbimm
Grimm glimm gnimm bimbimm
Grimm glimm gnimm bimbimm
Grimm glimm gnimm bimbimm

Bumm bimbimm   bamm bimbimm   11
Bumm bimbimm   bamm bimbimm
Bumm bimbimm   bamm bimbimm
Bumm bimbimm   bamm bimbimm

Grimm glimm gnimm bimbimm   11
Grimm glimm gnimm bimbimm
Grimm glimm gnimm bimbimm
Grimm glimm gnimm bimbimm

Bumm bimbimm   bamm bimbimm   **11**
Bumm bimbimm   bamm bimbimm
Bumm bimbimm   bamm bimbimm
Bumm bimbimm   bamm bimbimm

Bemm   bemm   **11**
Bemm   bemm
Bemm   bemm
Bemm   bemm

thema 12:   **12**
Tilla loola luula loola
Tilla luula loola luula
Tilla loola luula loola
Tilla luula loola luula

Grimm glimm gnimm bimbimm *(sehr kräftig beginnen)*   **11**
Grimm glimm gnimm bimbimm
Grimm glimm gnimm bimbimm
Grimm glimm gnimm bimbimm
Grimm glimm gnimm bimbimm
Grimm glimm gnimm bimbimm
Grimm glimm gnimm bimbimm
Grimm glimm gnimm bimbimm

Bumm bimbimm   bamm bimbimm   **11**
Bumm bimbimm   bamm bimbimm
Bumm bimbimm   bamm bimbimm
Bumm bimbimm   bamm bimbimm

Bemm   bemm   **11**
Bemm   bemm
Bemm   bemm
Bemm   bemm

thema 13:   **(Q)** **13**
Tatta tatta tuiEe tuiEe
Tatta tatta tuiEe tuiEe

Tatta tatta tuiEe tuiEe
Tatta tatta tuiEe tuiEe

thema 14:
Tilla lalla tilla lalla
Tilla lalla tilla lalla
Tilla lalla tilla lalla
Tilla lalla tilla lalla

14

Tuii tuii tuii tuii
Tuii tuii tuii tuii
Tee tee tee tee
Tee tee tee tee

13

Tuii tuii tuii tuii
Tuii tuii tuii tuii
Tee tee tee tee
Tee tee tee tee

Tatta tatta tuiEe tuiEe
Tatta tatta tuiEe tuiEe
Tatta tatta tuiEe tuiEe
Tatta tatta tuiEe tuiEe

13

Tilla lalla tilla lalla
Tilla lalla tilla lalla
Tilla lalla tilla lalla
Tilla lalla tilla lalla

14

Tuii tuii tuii tuii
Tuii tuii tuii tuii
Tee tee tee tee
Tee tee tee tee

13

Tuii tuii tuii tuii
Tuii tuii tuii tuii
Tee tee tee tee
Tee tee tee tee

Ooo bee ooo bee   6
Ooo bee ooo bee
Ooo bee ooo bee
Ooo bee ooo bee

(vierten teil von anfang bis hier wiederholen)   **(R) (S)**

durcharbeitung: **(T)**   6/1
Ooobee tatta tuu
Ooobee tatta tuu
Ooobee tatta tuii Ee
Ooobee tatta tuii Ee
Ooobee tatta tuiiEe tuiiEe
Ooobee tatta tuiiEe tuiiEe

Tatta tatta tuiiEe tuiiEe   13
Tatta tatta tuiiEe tuiiEe

Lümpff tümpff trill   13
Ziiuu lenn trill   3
Ziiuu lenn trill
Rrumpff tilff too   4

Rinnze kette bee   3
Rinnze kette bee
Rinnze kette bee bee
Rinnze kette bee bee
Rinnze kette beebee beebee
Rinnze kette beebee beebee

Rinnzekete beebee nnzkrr müü?   3
Ziiuu ennze ziiu rinnzkrrmüü
Rakete bee bee   3a

Grimme glimme gnimme bimme   11
Grimme glimme gnimme bimme
Grimme glimme gnimme bimme
Grimme glimme gnimme bimme

Graaaaa
Graaaaa   **15**

Grimme glimme gnimme bimme   **11**
Grimme glimme gnimme bimme
Grimme glimme gnimme bimme
Grimme glimme gnimme bimme

Graaaaa   **15**
Graaaaa

Ooobee tatta tee   **6/13**
Ooobee tatta tee
Ooobee tatta tee tee
Ooobee tatta tee tee
Ooobee tatta teetee teetee
Ooobee tatta teetee teetee
Ooobee tatta teeta tatta
Ooobee tatta teeta tatta

Tatta tatta teeta tatta
Tatta tatta teeta tatta   **13**

Ooobee tatta tuu   **6/13**
Ooobee tatta tuu
Ooobee tatta tuii Ee
Ooobee tatta tuii Ee
Ooobee tatta tuiiEe tuiiEe
Ooobee tatta tuiiEe tuiiEe

Tatta tatta tuiiEe tuiiEe   **13**
Tatta tatta tuiiEe tuiiEe

Tilla lalla tilla lalla   **14**
Tilla lalla tilla lalla

Tuii tuii tuii tuii   **13**
Tuii tuii tuii tuii
'Tee tee tee tee

LIVING UR SONATA

Tee tee tee tee
Tuii tuii tuii tuii
Tuii tuii tuii tuii
Tee tee tee tee
Tee tee tee tee

Ooo bee ooo bee
Ooo bee ooo bee
Ooo bee ooo bee
Ooo bee oooobee tatta

Grimme glimme gnimme bimme
Grimme glimme gnimme bimme
Grimme glimme gnimme bimme
Grimme glimme gnimme bimme

Tilla loola luula loola
Tilla loola luula loola

Grimme glimme gnimme bimme
Grimme glimme gnimme bimme
Grimme glimme gnimme bimme
Grimme glimme gnimme bimme

Tilla luula loola luula
Tilla luula loola luula

Loola luula loola luula
Loola luula loola luula
Luula loola luula loola
Luula loola luula loola

Luula luula luula luula
Loola loola loola loola
Loola loola loola loola
Luula luula luula luula

Ooobee tatta tuu
Ooobee tatta tuu

Ooobee tatta tuuta tatta
Ooobee tatta tuuta tatta

Tatta tatta tuuta tatta   13
Tatta tatta tuuta tatta
Tatta tatta tatta tatta
Tatta tatta tatta tatta

Rinnze ketta bee   3
Rinnze ketta bee
Rinnze ketta bee bee
Rinnze ketta bee bee
Rinnze ketta beebee beebee
Rinnze ketta beebee beebee

Beebee beebee beebee beebee   3
Beebee beebee beebee beebee

Tatta tatta tatta tatta
Tatta tatta tatta tatta

Grimme glimme gnimme bimme   11
Grimme glimme gnimme bimme

Graaaaa   graaaaa   15
Graaaaa   graaaaa

Lümpff tümpff trill   10
Ziiuu lenn trill   3
Ziiuu lenn trill
Rrumpff tilff too   4

EkeEke ekeEke ekeEke ekeEke   16
EkeEke ekeEke ekeEke ekeEke   16/4
EkeEke ekeEke Rrrumm!
EkeEke ekeEke Rrrumm!
EkeEke ekeEke Rrum Rrum
EkeEke ekeEke Rrum Rrum

Rrum Rrum Rrum Rrum
Rrum Rrum Rrum Rrum

ablösung (U)

Grimm glimm gnimm bimbimm
Grimm glimm gnimm bimbimm
Grimm glimm gnimm bimbimm
Grimm glimm gnimm bimbimm
Grimm glimm gnimm bimbimm
Grimm glimm gnimm bimbimm
Grimm glimm gnimm bimbimm
Grimm glimm gnimm bimbimm

Bumm bimbimm   bamm bimbimm
Bumm bimbimm   bamm bimbimm
Bumm bimbimm   bamm bimbimm
Bumm bimbimm   bamm bimbimm

Grimm glimm gnimm bimbimm
Grimm glimm gnimm bimbimm
Grimm glimm gnimm bimbimm
Grimm glimm gnimm bimbimm

Bumm bimbimm   bamm bimbimm
Bumm bimbimm   bamm bimbimm
Bumm bimbimm   bamm bimbimm
Bumm bimbimm   bamm bimbimm

Bemm   bemm
Bemm   bemm
Bemm   bemm
Bemm   bemm

Tilla loola luula loola
Tilla luula loola luula
Tilla loola luula loola
Tilla luula loola luula

Grimm glimm gnimm bimbimm *(sehr kräftig beginnen)*   **11**
Grimm glimm gnimm bimbimm
Grimm glimm gnimm bimbimm
Grimm glimm gnimm bimbimm
Grimm glimm gnimm bimbimm
Grimm glimm gnimm bimbimm
Grimm glimm gnimm bimbimm
Grimm glimm gnimm bimbimm

Bumm bimbimm   bamm bimbimm   **11**
Bumm bimbimm   bamm bimbimm
Bumm bimbimm   bamm bimbimm
Bumm bimbimm   bamm bimbimm

Bemm   bemm   **11**
Bemm   bemm
Bemm   bemm
Bemm   bemm

kadenz*(ad libitum) (an dieser stelle folgt die kadenz. die kadenz kann vom vortragenden aus teilen der ganzen sonate neu gestaltet werden. ich lasse statt dessen hier eine allgemeine kadenz mit neuen themen folgen)*

Priimittii   (V)   **17**
Priimiititti

Priimiititti too   **17**
Priimiititti taa
Priimiititti too
Priimiititti taa

Priimiititti tootaa   **17a**
Priimiititti tootaa
Priimiititti tuutaa
Priimiititti tuutaa

Priimiititti tootaatuu   **17a**

Priimiititti tootaatuu
Priimiititti tuutaatoo
Priimiititti tuutaatoo

Tatta tatta tuutaa too   13/17a
Tatta tatta tuutaa too

Tatta tatta tuiiEe tuiiEe   (W)
Tatta tatta tuiiEe tuiiEe
Tatta tatta tuiiEe tuiiEe
Tatta tatta tuiiEe tuiiEe

Tilla lalla tilla lalla   13
Tilla lalla tilla lalla
Tilla lalla tilla lalla
Tilla lalla tilla lalla

Tuii tuii tuii tuii   14
Tuii tuii tuii tuii
Tee tee tee tee
Tee tee tee tee

Tuii tuii tuii tuii
Tuii tuii tuii tuii
Tee tee tee tee
Tee tee tee tee

Tatta tatta tuiiEe tuiiEe   13
Tatta tatta tuiiEe tuiiEe
Tatta tatta tuiiEe tuiiEe
Tatta tatta tuiiEe tuiiEe

Tilla lalla tilla lalla   14
Tilla lalla tilla lalla
Tilla lalla tilla lalla
Tilla lalla tilla lalla

Tuii tuii tuii tuii   13
Tuii tuii tuii tuii

Tee tee tee tee
Tee tee tee tee

Tuii tuii tuii tuii
Tuii tuii tuii tuii
Tee tee tee tee
Tee tee tee tee

Ooo bee ooo bee   6
Ooo bee ooo bee
Ooo bee ooo bee
Ooo bee ooo bee

Ooooooooooooooooooooooooooooooooo   (X)   6

Dll Rrrrr bee bö   5

Fümms bö wö tää zää Uu,   1
                    pögiff,
                            müü

Rakete rinzekete   U 3
Rakete rinzekete   3 a
Rakete rinzekete
Rakete rinzekete
Rakete rinzekete
Rakete rinzekete

Bee   1
          bö
Böwö
          böwörö
Böwöböpö
          böwöröböpö
Böwörötääböpö
          böwörötääböpö
       tääböpö
             tüüböpö

tääböpö
    tüüböpö

Ooka ooka ooka ooka   8
Züüka züüka züüka züüka   9
Rmmp rnnf rmmp rnnf   4

Rumpftillfftoo?   Rrrrrrum!   4
Lanke trr gll?   Rrrrrrum!   III
Dedesnn nn rrrrr?   Rrrrrrum!   2

Mpiff tillff too?   Rrrrrrum!   2
Zikete bee bee?   Rrrrrrum!   3

Fö?   Rrrrrrum!   1
Ennze, ennze?   Rrrrrrum!   3

Rrumpfftilffto?   4
Bee bee bee bee bee   3a
Zee zee zee zee zee

Pe pe pe pe pe   8
Pii pii pii pii pii   9
Poo poo poo poo poooo?

Grimm glimm gnimm bimbimm *(mit starker betonung)*   11
Grimm glimm gnimm bimbimm
Grimm glimm gnimm bimbimm
Grimm glimm gnimm bimbimm
Grimm glimm gnimm bimbimm
Grimm glimm gnimm bimbimm
Grimm glimm gnimm bimbimm
Grimm glimm gnimm bimbimm

Ooo   bee *(sehr stark fallend)*   6
Ooo   bee
Ooo   bee
Ooo   bee

schluss:

Zätt üpsiilon iks *(bewegt)*   (Y) 18
Wee fau Uu
Tee äss ärr kuu
Pee Oo änn ämm
Ell kaa Ii haa
Gee äff Ee dee zee beee?

Zätt üpsiilon iks *(bewegter)*   18
Wee fau Uu
Tee äss ärr kuu
Pee Oo änn ämm
Ell kaa Ii haa
Gee äff Ee dee zee beee?

Zätt üpsiilon iks *(einfach)*   18a
Wee fau Uu
Tee äss ärr kuu
Pee Oo änn ämm
Ell kaa Ii haa
Gee äff Ee dee zee bee Aaaaa.

Zätt   *(sehr bewegt)*   (Z) 18
     üpsiilon iks
Wee fau Uu
Tee äss ärr kuu
Pee Oo änn ämm
Ell kaa Ii haa
Gee äff Eeee dee zee beeee? *(schmerzlich)*

ACKNOWLEDGMENTS

Thanks to *Ur Sonata* performance colleagues: Mitch Ahern, Jeff Beer, Karl Berger, Pronoblem (James Bickford), Miles Bickford, Valerie Caris Blitz, Eric Gonzalez-Blitz, Jenny Gonzalez-Blitz, Lynn Book, Andy Crespo, Philip Hart Helzer, Bob Holman, Johnse Holt, John Landino, Stephen Lindow, Denis Luzuriaga, Rebecca Migdal, Joe Morrella, Jack Nelson, Fly Orr, Amanda Petrovato, Brad Phillips, David Poppie, Don Rice, Steve Rice, DJ Glove (Joshua Selman), Ingrid Sertso, Bob Wilson, and Steve Wishnia.

Thanks to venues and arts programmers who presented us: 119 Gallery (Walter Wright), Anchor House of Artists (Michael Tillyer), Bowery Poetry Club (Bob Holman), Cabaret Voltaire (Harry Hoch), Chicago Academy of the Arts, Chicago Filmmakers (Robert Metrick, Brenda Webb), Club Lower Links (Leigh Jones), Clubhouse Studios (Paul Antonell, owner/sound-engineer), Easthampton Art Walk (Burns Maxey), El Taller Latino Americano (Bernardo Palombo), Emit Gallery, Grey Matter Books (Sam Burton), Mara Tapp, Latvian Booksellers Association (Inara Belinkaya, Ainars Roze), Montague Common Hall (Laura Roberts), Multi-Use Community Cultural Center (Doug Rice), Outpost 186 (Rob Chalfen), Phantom Brain Exchange @ The Rendezvous (Neil Young Cloaca), School of the Art Institute of Chicago (Lynn Book), Vox Pop (Debi Ryan), West Haven Parks, and Westbeth (Tamara Wyndham).

Thanks to my music mentors: Karl Berger, Mwata Bowden, Steve Carbonara, Ned Corman, Douglas Ewart, Vandy Harris, Kawase Junsuke, Alan Silva.

Thanks to my middle- and high-school German teachers: Fraulein Schnell and Herr Russell Webber.

Thanks to Dr Gwendolen Webster for kindly reviewing an early draft, alerting me to several errors, and then publishing four chapters in the Kurt Schwitters Society newsletter. Thanks also, for encouragement, to Dr Isabel Schulz, curator of Kurt Schwitters Archive at Sprengel Museum in Hannover.

Thanks to family: Claire Laties Davis, Nancy Laties Feresten, Tim Feresten, Martha Laties, Samuel Laties, Sarah Laties, Victor Laties, Christine Bluhm, Sylvan Migdal, Jessica Spears, and Curtis Whitear.

Special gratitude to my soulmate Rebecca Migdal for love and support, and for encouraging me—after a fourteen-year lapse—to resume performing *Ur Sonata*.

Thanks to Kurt Schwitters, for lifelong inspiration.

PHOTO & ART CREDITS

Jenny Gonzalez-Blitz, Brooklyn and Rhinebeck: 104, 105. Denis Luzuriaga, Holyoke, Manhattan, West Haven: 101, 102, 103, 104. Rebecca Migdal, Holyoke: 106. Peter Palombella, Holyoke: book cover, 102. Doug Rice, Rochester: 103. Ed Sacks, Chicago: 101.

NOTES

PREFACE

Page i. "The general sense of insecurity"
Gwendolen Webster. *Kurt Merz Schwitters, A Biographical Study*. Cardiff: University of Wales Press, 1997. 227.

Page ii. "Utopian 'supranationalist'"
Kurt Schwitters. "National Feeling," *Myself and My Aims*. Edited by Megan Luke, translated by Timothy Grundy. Chicago, IL: University of Chicago Press, 2021. 200.

Page ii. "personal mission to free words and letters"
"Merz wants freedom from any restraint, so that it can give form with artistic intent… The elements of poetry are letters, syllables, words, sentences. Evaluating these elements against each other makes poetry. Sense is necessary only when it is also evaluated as a factor. I evaluate sense against nonsense. I prefer nonsense, but that is a purely personal matter." Kurt Schwitters. "Merz," *Myself and My Aims: Writings on Art and Criticism*. Edited by Megan Luke, translated by Timothy Grundy. Chicago, IL: University of Chicago Press, 2021. 72.

Page ii. "abstract poetry evaluates"
Kurt Schwitters. "Artists' Right to Self-Determination," *Myself and My Aims*. Edited by Megan Luke, translated by Timothy Grundy. Chicago, IL: University of Chicago Press, 2021. 31-32.

Page iii. "Ball, like so many other artists"
Rasula, Jed. *Destruction was My Beatrice*. New York: Basic Books, 2015. 5.

Page iii. "The *Ursonate* is the most purely abstract."
Kurt Schwitters. "Myself and My Aims," *Myself and My Aims*. Edited by Megan Luke, translated by Timothy Grundy. Chicago, IL: University of Chicago Press, 2021. 417.

Page iv. *"Phonics Is Fun"*
Louis Krane. *Phonics Is Fun.* Berea, OH: Modern Curriculum
Press, 1963.

Page iv. "The Blues and the Abstract Truth"
Oliver Nelson. *The Blues and the Abstract Truth.* New York:
Impulse!, 1961.

Page v. "Adolf Hitler had himself photographed"
"The camera catches Hitler laughing…while standing in front of
a wall on which paintings by Wassily Kandinsky, Paul Klee, and
Kurt Schwitters are hanging, rather deliberately askew. Across
the top of the display runs a quote from George Grosz that
reads, 'Take Dada seriously! It's worth it.'"
Dave Hannigan. *Barbed Wire University.* Essex, CT: Lyons Press,
2021. 31.

Page v. "bourgeois and idiot"
Self-described: *Bürger und Idiot.* Written into Kate Steinitz's
guest book. Kate Trauman Steinitz. *Kurt Schwitters, A Portrait
from Life.* Berkeley/Los Angeles, CA: University of California
Press, 1968.

Page v. *"Meine Sonate in Urlauten"*
In English: Kurt Schwitters. "My Sonata in Primal Sounds,"
PPPPPP: Poems Performances Pieces Proses Plays Poetics. Edited
by Jerome Rothenberg and Pierre Joris Philadelphia, PA: Temple
University Press, 1993. German: Kurt Schwitters. *Kurt Schwitters.
Die literarischen Werke, 5,* edited by Friedhelm Lach. Koln:
Dumont, [1973] 1998. 288-292

CHAPTER ZÄTT—THEMES 17, 13, 12, 14, 6
Page 1. "Schwitters survives"
John Russell. *An Alternative Art,* The Meanings of Modern Art
series, Vol. 6. New York: Museum of Modern Art, 1974. 44.

Page 1. "Graphic journalist Rebecca Migdal"
"Rebecca Migdal is an author and an interdisciplinary artist working in new and traditional media. She has worked as a filmmaker, designer, teacher and performer." www.rlmigdal.com/resume. For instance: Rebecca Migdal, "Goddess Arise: An Incantation to Heal the Feminine," *My Body / Our Rights, World War 3 Illustrated #53.* Edited by Paula Hewitt Amram, Sabrina Jones, and Rebecca Migdal. Chico, CA: AK Press, 2023. 100-112.

CHAPTER ÜPSIILON

Page 9. "Nazi SA raided the office Paul Renner"
"A copy of Merz 24, containing the *Ursonate*, had...been seized by the SA and denounced as a Bolshevist work." Gwendolen Webster. *Kurt Merz Schwitters, A Biographical Study.* Cardiff: University of Wales Press, 1997. 252.

Page 9. "Jan Tschichold and his students"
"...Completed the typography of the whole sonata as a project with his students."—Gwendolen Webster. *Kurt Merz Schwitters, A Biographical Study.* Cardiff: University of Wales Press, 1997. 240.

Page 9. "Heavily-ligatured blackletter fonts"
"It was forbidden to use modern design or sans-serif typefaces such as Futura, which Goebbels called a 'Jewish invention.'" Steven Heller and Louise Fili, *German Modern: Graphic Design from Wilhelm to Weimar.* San Francisco, CA: Chronicle Books, 1998. 17.

Page 9. *"Die Neue Typographie"*
Jan Tschichold. *The New Typography* [1928], translated by Ruari McLean. Berkeley/Los Angeles, CA: University of California Press, 2006.

Page 9. *"Kulturbolschewismus: communism's advance-guard"*
In English, "Cultural Bolshevist."—Gwendolen Webster. *Kurt Merz Schwitters, A Biographical Study.* Cardiff: University of Wales Press, 1997. 250

Page 9. *"Ur Sonata ("Primeval Sonata")"*
Kurt Schwitters. *"Ursonate,"* Merz 24. Hannover: Merzverlag, 1932. Download: Kurt Schwitters, Kocher, Ursula and Schulz, Isabel. *Band 4 Die Reihe Merz 1923–1932*, Berlin, Boston: De Gruyter, 2019. 420-435. https://doi.org/10.1515/9783110624113. In English: Kurt Schwitters. *PPPPPP: Poems Performances Pieces Proses Plays Poetics.* Edited and translated by Jerome Rothenberg & Pierre Joris Philadelphia, PA: Temple University Press, 1993. 52-80.

Page 10. *"Eugene Jolas' Paris quarterly transition"*
Transition Workshop. Edited by Eugene Jolas. New York: Vanguard Press, 1949. 177.

Page 10. *"The font he'd created, Futura, was banned"*
Steven Heller and Louise Fili, *German Modern: Graphic Design from Wilhelm to Weimar.* San Francisco, CA: Chronicle Books, 1998. 17.

Page 10. *"Jan Tschichold was imprisoned"*
Paul Stirton. *Jan Tschichold and the New Typography: Graphic Design Between the World Wars.* New Haven, CT: Yale University Press, 2019. 164.

Page 10. *"Kurt Schwitters was dismissed"*
Paul Stirton. *Jan Tschichold and the New Typography: Graphic Design Between the World Wars.* New Haven, CT: Yale University Press, 2019. 165.

Page 10. *"Include Schwitters' typographically adventurous books and magazines in book-burnings"*

"In May 1933 books were burned publicly in various German towns including Hanover, where a lorryload of literature was consigned to the flames. Offending authors included Brecht, Rudolf Steiner, Einstein, Freud, Gide, Kafka, Upton Sinclair, Thomas Mann, Hemingway, Jack London, Hellen Keller and countless others. Schwitters's books too were burned, along with those by old friends from Dada days." Gwendolen Webster. *Kurt Merz Schwitters, A Biographical Study.* Cardiff: University of Wales Press, 1997. 252.

Page 10. "His works, and by extension his own person" Roger Cardinal and Gwendolen Webster. *Kurt Schwitters.* Ostfildern: Hatje Kantz, 2012. 16-17.

Page 11. "Simply indescribable trash"
"Uberwundene 'Kunst'" *Neues Volk* 3, Easter, 1935. 33-34 Cited in: Megan Luke. *Kurt Schwitters: Space, Image, Exile.* Chicago: University of Chicago Press, 2014. 10.

Page 11. "Enlivening his poetry lectures."
Harriet Janis and Rudi Blesch. *Collage, Personalities, Concepts, Techniques.* Philadelphia, 1962. 73. Cited in: Gwendolen Webster. *Kurt Merz Schwitters, A Biographical Study.* Cardiff: University of Wales Press, 1997. 257.

CHAPTER IKS—THEMES 1, 6
Page 13. "A nonsense poem called *Priimiittitti*"
Transition Workshop. Edited by Eugene Jolas. [Originally in *Transition* 3, June 1927.] New York: Vanguard Press, 1949. 177.

CHAPTER WEE
Page 15. "I felt liberated."
Kurt Schwitters. "Facts From My Life." *Myself and My Aims: Writings on Art and Criticism.* Edited by Megan Luke, translated

by Timothy Grundy. Chicago, IL: University of Chicago Press, 2021. 341-342.

Page 15. *"An Anna Blume"*
Kurt Schwitters. *PPPPPP: Poems Performances Pieces Proses Plays Poetics.* Edited by Jerome Rothenberg and Pierre Joris Philadelphia, PA: Temple University Press, 1993. 16.

Page 15. *"onto public-announcement street-columns"*
Gwendolen Webster, "Kurt Schwitters: Plans and Elevations," in *Schwitters Miró Arp,* edited by Dieter Buchhart. Munich: Prestel, 2016. 125.

Page 16. *"his 1918 Plakatgedichte"*
Raoul Hausmann. *"Kurt Schwitters wird Merz."* In Am Anfang war Dada, 63-71. Giessen, Germany: Anabas-Verlag, 1972. 65. Cited in: Luke, Megan. *Kurt Schwitters: Space, Image, Exile.* Chicago: University of Chicago Press, 2014. 250.

Page 16. *"It became a bit much"*
Raoul Hausmann. *Am Anfang war Dada.* Eds. Karl Riha and Günter Kämpf. Lahn-Giessen, Germany: Anabas, 1972. Cited in Rasula, Jed. *Destruction was My Beatrice: Dada and the Unmaking of the Twentieth Century.* New York: Basic Books, 2015. 107.

Page 16. *"The effort was cut short by Schwitters' illness"*
"Penury and illness involving both collaborators—Schwitters with a broken leg between October and Christmas 1946—put paid to the project."—Sarah Wilson. "Kurt Schwitters in England," *Baltic,* no. 4, Gateshead, 1999.

Page 16. *"PIN was published in 1962"*
Kurt Schwitters and Raoul Hausmann and the Story of PIN. Edited by Jasia Reichardt. London: Gaberbocchus Press, 1962.

Page 16. "Filmmakers Franciszka and Stefan Themerson"
"The Themersons were born in Poland, and in the 1930s led a vital film-making avant-garde in Warsaw. They also produced books for children together. In 1938 they moved to Paris, but their plans were disrupted by the war. By 1942 they were reunited in London, where they spent the rest of their lives. They founded Gaberbocchus Press in 1948."—*Themerson Archive, Volume 1, Letters and documents.* Edited by Jasia Reichardt and Nick Wadley. Boston, MA: MIT Press, 2020. 7.

Page 16. "The *PIN* book's promo copy read"
Themerson Archive, Volume 3, Gaberbocchus. Edited by Jasia Reichardt and Nick Wadley. Boston, MA: MIT Press, 2020. 139

Page 17. "Themersons' niece, Jasia Reichardt"
Memoir: Jasia Reichardt. *15 Journeys: Warsaw to London.* Funks Grove, IL: Dalkey Archive Press, 2012.

Page 17. "*Sgt. Pepper*"
The Beatles. *Sgt. Pepper's Lonely Hearts Club Band.* London: EMI, 1967.

Page 17. "Collaged album-cover"
"Blake recalled of the concept: 'I offered the idea that if they had just played a concert in the park, the cover could be a photograph of the group just after the concert with the crowd who had just watched the concert, watching them.' He added, 'If we did this by using cardboard cut-outs, it could be a magical crowd of whomever they wanted.'"—Patrick Humphries. "Picture Perfect." *Mojo Special Limited Edition: 1000 Days that Shook the World (The Psychedelic Beatles—April 1, 1965 to December 26, 1967).* London: Emap, 2002. 97.

Page 17. "Reichardt described collages"
"I guess it was 1955. I was sharing a flat with Richard Smith and he was friendly with Jasia Reichardt. Jasia's uncle and aunt were

called the Themersons, and they were friends with Kurt Schwitters. Dick knew about that world through Jasia, and he explained to me about Schwitters, and we talked about collage and then we were just playing, making some collages." Natalie Rudd. "Peter Blake on Pop Art, Elvis and the endless potential of collage." Thames & Hudson blog, June 10, 2021. https://thamesandhudson.com/news/peter-blake-collage/

Page 17. "White Album"
The Beatles. *The Beatles.* London: EMI, 1968. Usually referred to as "The White Album."

Page 17. "Salvage of Schwitters' third Merzbau"
Sarah Wilson. "Kurt Schwitters in England," *Baltic,* no. 4, Gateshead, 1999.

Page 18. "Shoes serve and wear out"
Dick Higgins. "Intending," *The Something Else Newsletter,* April 1966. Cited in Dick Higgins. *Intermedia, Fluxus and the Something Else Press.* Edited by Steve Clay and Ken Friedman. Catskill, NY: Siglio Press, 2018. 37.

Page 19. *"Monty Python's* very first episode."
Monty Python's Flying Circus. "Whither Canada?" Series 1, Episode 1. London: BBC1, October 5, 1969.

Page 20. "English Companion Wantee"
"Vivacious and with a sense of humour close to Kurt's own, she made extremely welcome company."–Gwendolen Webster. *Kurt Merz Schwitters, A Biographical Study.* Cardiff: University of Wales Press, 1997. 329.

Page 20. "Emerged from his coma to sign the paperwork"
Roger Cardinal and Gwendolen Webster. *Kurt Schwitters.* Ostfildern: Hatje Kantz, 2012. 35.

CHAPTER FAU—THEME 18

Page 21. "Performance-artist Lynn Book"

"Lynn Book is a transmedia artist whose adventurous work interrogates and theorizes Bodies—biological, physical, social, political, boundless."—"About," Lynn Book Website, Retrieved March 28, 2023. https://www.lynnbook.com/about

Page 22. "Frequently critical attitude"

"My quarrels with Schwitters were caused chiefly by the fact that I was a dadaist and an existentialist, and he was an artist and nothing but an artist.... Schwitters was a highly talented petty bourgeois, one of those ingenious rationalists who smell of home cooking, who come pouring out of the German woods.... Our goals in Berlin were higher and different. We loved to hunt down people, we loved the malice of cheaters, the false prayers of murderers, and the dust that collects on the breasts of dead whores. What good was *Anna Blume*, in back, in front, I love you not, and it would have been better to nip the bloom in the bud."—Richard Huelsenbeck. *Memoirs of a Dada Drummer.* Translated by Joachim Neugroschel. Berkeley/Los Angeles, CA: University of California Press, 1969. 64.

Page 23. "Two kinds of dada"

"At this point I must mention Dadaism, which, like me, cultivates nonsense. There are two groups of Dadaists, the Core- and the Husk-Dadas, with the latter residing in Germany, for the most part. Initially there were just the Core-Dadaists before the Husk-Dadaists under their leader Huelsenbeck split away from the original core, peeling off parts of the core in the process. This peeling away was accompanied by loud howls, continuous singing of the Marseillaise, by doling out kicks with the elbows— a tactic Huelsenbeck employs to this day. Under Huelsenbeck, Dada became a political concern. The famous manifesto of the revolutionary German Central Council for Dada calls for radical communism as a Dadaist demand."–Kurt Schwitters. "Merz," *Myself and My Aims: Writings on Art and Criticism*. Edited by Megan Luke, translated by Timothy Grundy. Chicago, IL: University of Chicago Press, 2021. 72-73.

Page 23. "Merz, a one-man apolitical movement"
The definition of Merz evolved.
1919: "The word 'Merz' refers, essentially, to the embrace of all conceivable materials for artistic purposes and, technically, to the equal evaluation [*Wertung*] of individual materials as a matter of principle."–Kurt Schwitters. "Merz-Painting," *Myself and My Aims: Writings on Art and Criticism*. Edited by Megan Luke, translated by Timothy Grundy. Chicago, IL: University of Chicago Press, 2021. 24.

1926: From the standpoint that I call Merz, there are three requirements:

1) Human beings cannot create anything in accordance with the spirit of the almighty divinity. They cannot create nothing out of nothing, rather they can merely create out of definite givens, out of definite material. The act of human creating is only a process of forming that which is given.
2) Perfection [completeness] cannot be attained by human beings.
3) In his work the artist seeks to strive only for that which he can attain. Added to that comes the serious striving to make everything so good, so honest, so open and so logical as possible. The result from all this is Merz.

Merz is the smile at the grave and seriousness on cheerful occasions.

Kurt Schwitters. *Kurt Schwitters. Die literarischen Werke, 5,*
edited by Friedhelm Lach. Koln: Dumont, (1973) 1998. 144.
Cited in: Jack Zipes. "Kurt Schwitters, Politics, and the Merz
Fairy Tale," in *Lucky Hans and other Merz Fairy Tales,* by Kurt
Schwitters, translated by Jack Zipes. Princeton, NJ: Princeton
University Press, 2009. 30.

Page 23. "Nations exist, unfortunately"
Kurt Schwitters. "National Art." *Myself and My Aims: Writings
on Art and Criticism.* Edited by Megan Luke, translated by
Timothy Grundy. Chicago, IL: University of Chicago Press, 2021.
202.

Page 24. "Gaberbocchus Common Room"
In-person lecture: "Stefan Themerson presents Kurt Schwitters'
Last Notebook," February 25th, 1958. Published in: Stefan
Themerson. *Kurt Schwitters in England.* London: Gaberbocchus
Press. 1958. 14. On the Common Room: "August 1957. The aim
of this Common Room is to provide artists and scientists and
people interested in both the philosophy of science and the
philosophy of art with a congenial place where they can meet
and exchange thoughts.... It seems that the artificial barrier
dividing science from the arts is becoming obsolete and it may
be worth while to try to ignore it."—Stefan Themerson,
"Gaberbocchus Common Room," *Themerson Archive, Volume 3,
Gaberbocchus.* Edited by Jasia Reichardt and Nick Wadley.
Boston, MA: MIT Press, 2020. 205.

Page 24. "Blue is the colour of thy yellow hair"
From Kurt Schwitters' "Anna Blossom Has Wheels" ("An Anna
Blume").—Kurt Schwitters. *PPPPPP: Poems Performances Pieces
Proses Plays Poetics.* Edited by Jerome Rothenberg and Pierre
Joris Philadelphia, PA: Temple University Press, 1993. 16.

Page 25. "Symmetries and rhythms instead of principles"
Hugo Ball. *Fragments from a Dada Diary, 3, March 1916.*
Quoted from *Transition No. 25.* Cited in: Stefan Themerson. *Kurt Schwitters in England.* London: Gaberbocchus Press. 1958. 14.

Page 25. "Ernst joined the Socialist Workers' Youth"
Kurt Schwitters. *Myself and My Aims: Writings on Art and Criticism.* Edited by Megan Luke, translated by Timothy Grundy. Chicago, IL: University of Chicago Press, 2021. 440. Also: Gwendolen Webster. *Kurt Merz Schwitters, A Biographical Study.* Cardiff: University of Wales Press, 1997. 243.

CHAPTER UU
Page 27. "Original context a middle syllable"
Stefan Themerson. *Kurt Schwitters in England.* London: Gaberbocchus Press, 1958. 20.

Page 27. "Refers to Mercury"
"...[Schwitters'] relations with Mercury—commerce, Merz—were alas less well ordered."—Michael Hoffmann. *Where Have You Been? Selected Essays.* New York: Farrar Straus and Giroux, 2014. 237.

Page 28. "The time of birth" ... "Seek your good fortune within"
Kurt Schwitters, "Facts From My Life," in Kurt Schwitter, *Myself and My Aims: Writings on Art and Criticism.* Edited by Megan Luke, translated by Timothy Grundy. Chicago, IL: University of Chicago Press, 2021. 236. Kurt Schwitters, "Good or Bad Fortune," in Kurt Schwitter, *Myself and My Aims: Writings on Art and Criticism.* Edited by Megan Luke, translated by Timothy Grundy. Chicago, IL: University of Chicago Press, 2021. 298

Page 28. "Mad Hatter, of *Alice in Wonderland*"
Charles Dodgson (writing as Lewis Carroll). "Chapter 7, A Mad Tea-Party," *Alice's Adventures in Wonderland.* London, 1865.

Page 28. "Kurt Schwitters always used cinnabar"
"...The works were occasionally unsigned, when Schwitters could not find vermilion for his characteristic `KS' signature— surely a mark by which he wished these paintings to be recognised and distinguished from local productions or his own unfinished exercises.... See letter from Klaus Hinrichsen, to a Mrs Kassabian at Phillips (Wantee archives): `Schwitters insisted on signing and dating with Vermilion paint which in 1945 was unobtainable in the Lake District'."—Sarah Wilson. "Kurt Schwitters in England," *Baltic*, no. 4, Gateshead, 1999.

Page 28. "Cofounded Hannover *Zinnoberfest*"
Kate Trauman Steinitz. *Kurt Schwitters, A Portrait from Life.* Berkeley/Los Angeles, CA: University of California Press, 1968. 55.

Page 29. "Municipal cultural office resurrected *Zinnober*"
"Hannover Art Scene: Zinnober Current," Hannover Municipal Website, Retrieved March 28, 2023.
https://www.hannover.de/Kultur-Freizeit/Museen-Ausstellungen/Bildende-Kunst/ZINNOBER/ZINNOBER-Aktuell

CHAPTER TEE

Page 31. "Bring Your Own Restaurant"
"'You don't get invited; you just show up,' Bickford told us six years ago, at a BYOR at an abandoned gas station. 'It's not a club; it's not a party; it's about being neighbors.'"—Jill Kaufman. "'Bring Your Own Restaurant' Hot In Holyoke," *Morning Edition.* Washington DC: National Public Radio, October 21, 2010.
https://www.npr.org/templates/story/story.php?storyId=130679624

Page 33. "Valerie Caris Blitz"
"Influenced by 'all the disciplines of the 20th-century avant-garde,' she was heavily involved with the Lower East Side art

space ABC No Rio in its early days, exhibiting her paintings and performing there. She also spent time in Berlin, where eccentric art dealer Emanuela Schwankl organized her first solo show. She appeared in more than 40 films, including Ari Roussimoff's *Shadows of the City* and Michael Brynntrup's *Die Bortschaft* (The Message). After she was diagnosed with HIV in 1989, her work became more conceptual. Her pieces "Queen Sex Positive" and "Vestment" were part of the *Sur Rodney Sur* show "Blood Fairies." In the last 10 years, she returned to her first love, abstract-expressionist painting.—"A Life of Art and Activism Comes to an End," *The Indypendent.* August 13, 2009. https://indypendent.org/2009/08/a-life-of-art-and-activism-comes-to-an-end/

CHAPTER ÄSS

Page 35. "Magical exaltation of the object"
Carl Jung and Aniela Jaffé, *Man and His Symbols.* New York: Doubleday, 1964. 253.

Page 36. "One-man show in 1944"
"Berlin-born Jack Bilbo [Hugo Baruch] founded the Modern Art Gallery in 1941. Schwitters was joined by Simon Schames, Schiele, Kokoschka and a mixture of modern masters in his first group show. See *Jack Bilbo. An autobiography,* London, the Modern Art Gallery, 1948, pp 259 and 264, where Schwitters' recital is described part of a group evening in Bilbo's first premises."—Sarah Wilson. "Kurt Schwitters in England," *Baltic,* no. 4, Gateshead, 1999.

Page 36. "Introduction to the Schwitters exhibition catalog"
Herbert Read. "Preface," in *Paintings and Sculptures by Kurt Schwitters,* London: The Modern Art Gallery, 1944. Cited in: Sarah Wilson. "Kurt Schwitters in England," *Baltic,* no. 4, Gateshead, 1999. Also cited in Gwendolen Webster. *Kurt Merz*

Schwitters, A Biographical Study. Cardiff: University of Wales Press, 1997. 377.

Page 37. "Schwitters was so pleased"
Gwendolen Webster. *Kurt Merz Schwitters, A Biographical Study.* Cardiff: University of Wales Press, 1997. 343.

CHAPTER ÄRR—THEMES 11, 15, 16
Page 40. "Summer shows at Cabaret Voltaire"
Marla Donato. "Across from the car wash, their heart belongs to dada." *Chicago Tribune*, June 8th, 1988.
https://www.chicagotribune.com/news/ct-xpm-1988-06-08-8801050817-story.html

Page 41. *"Eli, Eli, lama sabachtani?"*
"My God, My God, why have You forsaken me?" Matthew (27:46)

CHAPTER KUU
Page 43. "If that's art, I'm a Hottentot,"
Jennifer Dasal. *Artcurious: Stories of the Unexpected, Slightly Odd, and Strangely Wonderful in Art History.* New York: Penguin Books, 2020. 27.

Page 43. "I don't pretend to be an artist or a judge of art"
Alfred Barr, Jr. "Is Modern Art Communistic?; On the contrary, says an expert, it is damned in Soviet Russia as it was in Nazi Germany." *The New York Times Magazine*, 1952.

Page 43. "Solicited three thousand dollars"
Adrian Sudhalter. "Kurt Schwitters and The Museum of Modern Art." Paper presented at "Kurt Schwitters and the Avant-Garde: International Symposium." Hannover: Sprengel Museum, 2007.

Page 45. "The Central Intelligence Agency was secret founder"
Hugh Wilford. *The Mighty Wurlitzer: How the CIA Played America.* Cambridge, MA: Harvard University Press, 2008. 101-

104. The phrase "free enterprise painting" is Nelson Rockefeller's; at the time he was MOMA's board chair.

Page 45. "Porter McCray"
Porter McCray. "American Tutti-Frutti," *E-flux Journal #60*, December 2014.
https://www.e-flux.com/journal/60/61041/american-tutti-frutti/

Page 45. "Scathing article in a 1952 issue"
Alfred Barr, Jr. "Is Modern Art Communistic?; On the contrary, says an expert, it is damned in Soviet Russia as it was in Nazi Germany." *The New York Times Magazine*, 1952.

CHAPTER PEE—THEME 5
Page 47. "My memoir, *Rebel Bookseller*"
Andrew Laties. "Chapter 6, Trading Places," *Rebel Bookseller: Why Indie Businesses Represent Everything You Want to Fight For—from Free Speech to Buying Local to Building Communities*, 2nd ed. New York: Seven Stories Press, 2011. 133.

Page 49. *"Das Grosse Lalula"*
Das Grosse Lalula

Kroklokwafzi? Semememi!
Seiokrontro - prafriplo:
Bifzi, bafzi; hulalemi;
quasti basti bo ...
Lalu lalu lalu lalu la!

Hontraruru miromente
zasku zes rü rü?
Entepente, leiolente
klekwapufzi lü?
Lalu lalu lalu lalu la!

Simarar kos malzipempu
silzuzankunkrei (;)!

Marjomar dos: Quempu Lempu
Siri Suri Sei ( )!
Lalu lalu lalu lalu la!

Christian Morgenstern. *Songs from the Gallows: Galgenlieder*, translated by Walter Arndt. New Haven, CT: Yale University Press, 1993.

CHAPTER OO—THEME 4

Page 51. "Bob Holman"
See: Bob Krasner, "The Spoken Word of Bob Holman, the globe-trotting unofficial poet laureate of the Lower East Side," *The Villager*, March 15, 2023.
https://www.amny.com/new-york/manhattan/bob-holman-globe-trotting-poet-lower-east-side/

Page 52. "Fluxus co-founder Alison Knowles"
"Visual artist known for her soundworks, installations, performances, publications and association with Fluxus, the experimental avant-garde group formally founded in 1962.—"Alison Knowles," Alison Knowles Website, Retrieved March 28, 2023. https://www.aknowles.com/

CHAPTER ÄNN

Page 53. "I can not agree that I should pray"
Kurt Schwitters. *Wir Spielen bis uns die Tod abholt, Briefen aus Fünf Jahrzeiten.* Edited by Ernst Nündel. Franfurt/M: Verlag Ullstein, 1974. 161.2.

Page 53. "Garden with roses, strawberries"
Kurt Schwitters. *Das Literarische Werk*, Vol. 5, *Manifeste und Kritische Prosa.* ed. Friedhelm Lach. Cologne, 1973-81. 83.
See: Kurt Schwitters. "Kurt Schwitters," *Myself and My Aims: Writings on Art and Criticism.* Edited by Megan Luke, translated by Timothy Grundy. Chicago, IL: University of Chicago Press, 2021. 66.

Page 54. "Art historian Jonathan Fineberg asks"
Jonathan Fineberg. "Schwitters: Tending the Enchanted
Garden," *Kurt Schwitters*, Zurich: Galerie Gmurzynska, 2016.
85.

Page 55. "Epilepsy as a condition to be eradicated"
P. Weindling. *Health, Race and German Politics Between
National Unification and Nazism, 1870-1945.* Cambridge:
Cambridge University Press, 1989. 525-526. Cited in: Clare
O'Dowd. "Kurt Schwitters' Merzbau: Chaos, Compulsion and
Creativity," *Movable Type,* Volume 5, "Mess," 2009.

Page 55. *"Die Zwiebel"*
Kurt Schwitters. *PPPPPP: Poems Performances Pieces Proses
Plays Poetics.* Edited by Jerome Rothenberg and Pierre Joris
Philadelphia, PA: Temple University Press, 1993. 121.

Page 55. "Hutchinson Internment Camp"
See: Simon Parkin. *The Island of Extraordinary Captives.* New
York: Simon & Schuster, 2022.

Page 55. "I go to our church"
Kurt Schwitters. *Wir Spielen bis uns die Tod abholt, Briefen aus
Fünf Jahrzeiten.* Edited by Ernst Nündel. Franfurt/M: Verlag
Ullstein, 1974. 161-2.

CHAPTER ÄMM—THEME 1
Page 57. "Eberhard Blum"
"A leading exponent of new and experimental instrumental,
vocal–verbal, conceptual, and interdisciplinary works."
"Eberhard Blum.org," Eberhard Blum Website, Retrieved March
28, 2023. https://www.eberhardblum.org/eberhardblum-org-
english/eberhard-blum/

Page 57. "Peter Froehlich"
"Peter Froehlich's play MERZ premiered in 1975 on the Fringe
of the Edinburgh Festival…. Froehlich has toured MERZ to

theatres, galleries, jazz clubs and concert halls across Canada, the US, Peru and Transylvania."—"Peter Froehlich's award-winning show MERZ reprised for GCTC fundraiser," Ottawa Festivals Website, Retrieved March 28, 2023. https://www.ottawafestivals.ca/peter-froehlichs-award-winning-show-merz-reprised-for-gctc-fundraiser/

Page 57. "Richard Kostelanetz"
Text-Sound Texts. Edited by Richard Kostelanetz. New York: William Morrow, 1980. 17.

Page 57. "Tesch, Haisch, Tschiiaa; Haisch, Tschiiaa."
Kate Trauman Steinitz. "Fury of Sneezing," Kurt Schwitters, in *Kurt Schwitters, A Portrait from Life.* Berkeley/Los Angeles, CA: University of California Press, 1968. 105.

Page 58. "Lewis Carroll's nonsense poem"
Charles Dodgson, writing as Lewis Carroll. *The Hunting of the Snark.* London, 1875.

Page 59. "Sheep's Clothing"
"According to Martin Bresnick, a professor of composition and Coordinator of Yale School of Music's Composition Department, the tradition of all-night music festivals at Yale dates back to the 1970s. In 1977, Bresnick, who was then teaching 'Theory and Composition' in the Department of Music, started a music performing group called 'Sheep's Clothing.'"—Carrie Zhou. "Yale's all-night music fest revived at Murray." *Yale Daily News,* January 12, 2020. https://yaledailynews.com/blog/2020/01/12/yales-all-night-music-fest-revived-at-murray/

CHAPTER ELL—THEMES 8, 9, 10
Page 61. "Dada, Dada, Ursonate"
Andrew Laties, "Dada, Dada, Ursonate," press release. Chicago: The Children's Bookstore, 1992.

Page 62. "Ernst Schwitters wrote"
Ernst Schwitters. "Kurt Schwitters as writer, poet and lecturer," *Kurt Schwitters*. Zurich: Galerie Gmurzynska, 2016. 35.

CHAPTER KAA—THEME 1

Page 65. "He yelled, he sniffled, he barked"
Kate Steinitz. "Kurt Schwitters: A Portrait from Life," in *Montage, Satire and Cultism: Germany Between the Wars*. Ed. by Herbert Knust. Champaign, IL: University of Illinois Press, 1973. 2.

Page 65. "Dada Invasion of West Haven"
"Back in 1988 and a bunch of crazy kids invaded a beach at Lighthouse Park as Dadaists, 28 [sic] years later a bunch of crazy adults invade a beach in West Haven!!.... Artists streamed in from far and wide, including nearly a dozen designated "reunionists" who invaded the first time, back in '88. Why? 'It's Dada,' Landino says."—Sean Corvino and Doug Dangermon. *Dadaist Invasion of West Haven. Youtube*, posted September 12, 2016. https://youtu.be/wdLDltnw_fl

CHAPTER II—THEME 3

Page 73. "I heard Schwitters practicing his *Lautsonate*"
"*Er zischte, sauste, zirpte, flötete, gurrte, buchstabierte.*" Werner Schmalenbach. *Kurt Schwitters*. New York: Abrams, 1967. Cited by: Astrid Seme. "Urbirds Singing the Ursonate," *Tonspur* 41. 2010. https://tonspur.at/soundworks/astrid-seme/?lang=en. Retrieved May 6, 2023.

Page 74. "*World War 3 Illustrated*"
See: *World War 3 Illustrated: 1979-2014*. Edited by Peter Kuper and Seth Tobocman. Binghamton, NY: PM Press, 2014.

Page 74. "Had to withdraw their records"
Jaap Blonk: "When in 1986 I made my first recording of the piece, for an LP to be issued by Willem Breuker's BVHaast label, I wrote to the publishers of Schwitters' work, Dumont Verlag in

Cologne, to ask for permission. No answer came, and after a second letter for more than six months no answer came, and then Breuker decided to issue the record anyway. But then at last a very angry letter arrived, written by a lawyer of Dumont Verlag upon orders of Ernst, the son of Kurt Schwitters. It turned out that Ernst had been on a journey in the Pacific and had not seen my letters until much later. The letter said that the record was illegal and all the copies had to be destroyed. After an extended legal correspondence it didn't get as far as destruction, but still the record could not be sold in shops anymore. Apparently Ernst Schwitters was convinced that the only genuine version of the Ursonate could be by his father. When the Swiss label Hat Hut Records issued a version by Eberhard Blum, they were taken to court and selling the recording was prohibited in Germany. Although I, and many people with me, thought that this recording ban was very much against Kurt Schwitters' spirit (he had encouraged people to perform the Ursonate and even written instructions for them!), nothing could be done against it until 2002, when Schwitters' grandson Bengt helped in founding the 'Kurt und Ernst Schwitters Stiftung' in Hannover (Ernst Schwitters had died in 1996). From then on the ban was lifted and permissions could be given to issue recordings."—Jaap Blonk, "Some words to Kurt Schwitters' URSONATE, by Jaap Blonk." Jaap Blonk Website, Retrieved April 3, 2023.
http://www.jaapblonk.com/Texts/ursonatewords.html

Page 74. "Ernst said you had to perform like Kurt"
Here is Kurt Schwitters (writing in English not German), contradicting his son Ernst's later attitude: "I do sound poems, and the key gives the manner how I would read them and as anybody <u>could</u> read them…. Of course, it may be read quite different[ly]. The translation gives only one key of reading it." Kurt Schwitters. "Key for Reading Sound Poems," *Myself and*

My Aims: Writings on Art and Criticism. Edited by Megan Luke, translated by Timothy Grundy. Chicago, IL: University of Chicago Press, 2021. 477.

Page 74. "John Coltrane"
John Coltrane. *My Favorite Things.* New York: Atlantic Records, 1961.

Page 74. "Julie Andrews"
The Sound of Music. Directed by Robert Wise, starring Julie Andrew. Argyle Enterprises, 1965.

Page 74. "Kurt on Youtube"
Kurt Schwitters Ursonate 1932, Youtube.
https://youtu.be/1qLKu3R8no4

CHAPTER HAA
Page 77. "How to accomplish this"
Ernst Schwitters. "Kurt Schwitters as writer, poet and lecturer," *Kurt Schwitters.* Zurich: Galerie Gmurzynska, 2016. 35.

Page 78. "Biographer Gwendolen Webster notes"
Gwendolen Webster. *Kurt Merz Schwitters, A Biographical Study.* Cardiff: University of Wales Press, 1997. 163.
Merz 13 is Online at:
https://media.sas.upenn.edu/pennsound/authors/Schwitters/Sc
hwitters-Kurt_01_Sonate-in-Urlauten_Urwerk_2007.mp3

Page 78. "Art historian Kevin Concannon"
Kevin Concannon. "Cut and Paste: Collage and the Art of Sound," in *Sound by Artists.* Banff, Canada: Art Metropole and Walter Phillips Gallery, 1990.
https://www.ubu.com/papers/concannon.html

Page 78. "Southern German Broadcasting Company"
This 1932 recording is online at:
https://media.sas.upenn.edu/pennsound/authors/Schwitters/Sc
hwitters-Kurt_14_Ursonate-Kurzfassung_Urwerk_2007.mp3

Page 79. "Sixteen people, including two journalists."
Kurt Schwitters. *Three Stories, with a Tribute by E.L.T. Mesens.*
Edited by Jasia Reichardt. London: Tate Publishing, 2010. 16.

Page 79. "Stefan Themerson was also there"
Stefan Themerson. *Kurt Schwitters in England.* London:
Gaberbocchus Press, 1958. 28.

Page 79. "Hannover 'Cathedral of Erotic Misery'"
Gwendolen Webster. "Hidden Meanings: The Merzbau," *Kurt
Merz Schwitters, A Biographical Study.* Cardiff: University of
Wales Press, 1997. 208-225.

CHAPTER GEE—THEMES 6, 7
Page 82. "Karl Berger's Creative Improvisers Orchestra"
"CMS [Creative Music Studio] and its artistic director, Karl
Berger, have pioneered an innovative way of blending the
sounds of improvising musicians... The groups are comprised of
leading professional string, horn, reed, vocalists and
percussionists who are conducted in live improvised
performances."—"Improvisers Performances," Creative Music
Studio Website, Retrieved March 28, 2013.
https://creativemusic.org/programs/improvisers-orchestra/

CHAPTER ÄFF
Page 85. "Filled it with guinea pigs"
Paul Bowles. *Without Stopping: An Autobiography.* New York:
Ecco Press, 1972. 115.

Page 86. "Assembling another *Merzbau*"
"When he moved to Norway permanently, Schwitters began
a...*Merzbau* in a small wooden house behind his main home in

Lysaker, near Oslo. Fleeing to Britain in 1940, he also left this construction unfinished. Fire destroyed it in 1951."
"Kurt Schwitters' Merz Barn Wall," Hatton Gallery Website, Retrieved March 27, 2023.
https://hattongallery.org.uk/collections/kurt-schwitters-merz-barn-wall

Page 86. "He did have a seizure later"
Gwendolen Webster. *Kurt Merz Schwitters, A Biographical Study*. Cardiff: University of Wales Press, 1997. 307.

Page 86. "Biographer Gwendolen Webster relates"
Georg Muche. *Blickppunkt Sturm, Dada, Bauhaus, Gegenwart*. Munich, 1961. 178. Cited in: Gwendolen Webster. *Kurt Merz Schwitters, A Biographical Study*. Cardiff: University of Wales Press, 1997. 301.

Page 87. "A starling uttering strange sounds"
Wolfgang Müller. *Hausmusik Stare aus Hjertøya singen Kurt Schwitters*. Berlin: Wolfgang Müller and Galerie Katze 5 Röske & Schumacher GbR, 2000.

CHAPTER EEE—THEME 2
Page 91. *"Art in Chicago, 1945-1995"*
"Out of the performance-art lineage, Lynn Book and Andy Lateis [sic] developed a highly theatrical version of Dadaist Kurt Schwitters' sound poem *Ursonate*."—Jeff Corbett, "Sonic Shards: Chicago's Sonic Arts," in *Art in Chicago, 1945-1995*. Organized by Lynne Warren. New York: Thames & Hudson, 1996. 120.

CHAPTER DEE—THEMES 3, 11
Page 93. "We play until death comes to fetch us"
"Kurt Schwitters, Letter to Christof Spengemann, July 24, 1946," Ernst Nündel, *Kurt Schwitters, Wir spielen bis uns der Tod*

abholt: Briefe aus fünf Jahrzehnten. Frankfurt/M: Ullstein. 1974. 210.

Page 93. "Swirls, projected from *Youtube*"
"The classic Sonata In Primeval Sounds, also called Ursonate by Kurt Schwitters (1922-32) as performed by pronoblem - text to speech synth, FluxBoard, two bass tracks (same track, once forward and again manipulated - stretched, compressed, reveresed, etc) and tenor sax."—Pronoblem (James Bickford). *Ursonate (edit). Youtube,* posted July 13, 2009. https://youtu.be/PvWi6rJ9N4o

Page 94. "Officially designated it James Bickford day"
"Bickford would smack politicians and others prominent in the community he felt were failing to do their jobs…. At the same time that Bickford would give rides to people whose vehicles were in the shop, cook meals for someone facing a hardship, hold marathon board-game sessions at his home here and discuss art, music and books because he'd seemingly read everything." Mike Plaisance. "Activist James Bickford recalled as friend, impatient agitator, lover of Holyoke." *Springfield Republican,* September 16, 2016. www.masslive.com/news/2016/09/post_748.html

CHAPTER ZEE—THEME 18
Page 95. "New issue of *World War 3 Illustrated*"
Fight Fascism! World War 3 Illustrated #48. Edited by Seth Tobocman et al. Chico, CA: AK Press, 2017.

CHAPTER BEEEE?—THEME 1
Page 97. "*Pennsound's Kurt Schwitters webpage*"
"Kurt Schwitters: The Ursonate (or: Sonate in Urlauten), 1922-1932," *Pennsound* Website, Center for Programs in Contemporary Writing at the University of Pennsylvania. Retrieved March 27, 2023.

https://writing.upenn.edu/pennsound/x/Schwitters.php

Page 98. "Creative Music Studio"
"In 1971 musicians Karl Berger, Ingrid Sertso and Ornette Coleman founded the Creative Music Foundation. Its initial advisory board, comprised of legends from all aspects of music, the arts and philosophy, included composer John Cage, conductor/musician Gil Evans, philosopher/educator Buckminster Fuller, composer George Russell, painter Willem DeKooning and composer/conductor Gunther Schuller. Their goal was to establish a nonprofit organization focused on improvisation and musical cross-pollination that complemented musicians' academic studies."—"History," Creative Music Studio Website, Retrieved March 27, 2023. https://creativemusic.org/about/history

Page 98. "The Three Fates"
Listen to this recording at: *Urchestra. The Three Fates Sing Ur Sonata by Kurt Schwitters.* Bandcamp, April 7, 2023. https://urchestra.bandcamp.com/album/the-three-fates-sing-ur-sonata-by-kurt-schwitters-featuring-karl-berger-ingrid-sertso. This was one of Karl Berger's last recording sessions; he passed away Sunday, April 9, 2023.

UR SONATA, BY KURT SCHWITTERS
Page 108. *"Ursonate"*
Kurt Schwitters. "Ursonate," Merz 24. Hannover: Merzverlag, 1932. Download: Kurt Schwitters, Kocher, Ursula and Schulz, Isabel. *Band 4 Die Reihe Merz 1923–1932*, Berlin, Boston: De Gruyter, 2019. 420-435. https://doi.org/10.1515/9783110624113

BIBLIOGRAPHY

PERIODICALS & PAPERS

Barr, Alfred, Jr. "Is Modern Art Communistic?; On the contrary, says an expert, it is damned in Soviet Russia as it was in Nazi Germany." *The New York Times Magazine*, 1952.

Sudhalter, Adrian. "Kurt Schwitters and The Museum of Modern Art." Paper presented at "Kurt Schwitters and the Avante-Garde: International Symposium." Hannover: Sprengel Museum, 2007.

Wilson, Sarah. "Kurt Schwitters in England," *Baltic*, no. 4, Gateshead, 1999.

BOOKS

Bowles, Paul. *Without Stopping: An Autobiography*. New York: Ecco Press, 1972.

Cardinal, Roger and Gwendolen Webster. *Kurt Schwitters*. Ostfildern: Hatje Kantz, 2012.

Dasal, Jennifer. Artcurious: *Stories of the Unexpected, Slightly Odd, and Strangely Wonderful in Art History*. New York: Penguin Books, 2020.

Fight Fascism! World War 3 Illustrated #48. Edited by Seth Tobocman et al. Chico, CA: AK Press, 2017.

Hannigan, Dave. *Barbed Wire University*. Essex, CT: Lyons Press, 2021.

Hausmann, Raoul. *Am Anfang war Dada*. Eds. Karl Riha and Günter Kämpf. Lahn-Giessen, Germany: Anabas, 1972.

Hausmann, Raoul and Kurt Schwitters, *PIN and the Story of PIN*. London: Gaberbocchus Press, 1962.

Higgins, Dick. *Intermedia, Fluxus and the Something Else Press.* Edited by Steve Clay and Ken Friedman. Catskill, NY: Siglio Press, 2018.

Huelsenbeck, Richard. *Memoirs of a Dada Drummer.* Translated by Joachim Neugroschel. Berkeley/Los Angeles, CA: University of California Press, 1969.

Janis, Harriet and Rudi Blesch. *Collage, Personalities, Concepts, Techniques.* Philadelphia, 1962.

Kurt Schwitters. MERZ. Zurich: Galerie Gmurzynska, 2016.

Laties, Andrew. *Rebel Bookseller: Why Indie Businesses Represent Everything You Want to Fight For—from Free Speech to Buying Local to Building Communities,* 2nd ed. New York: Seven Stories Press, 2011.

Luke, Megan. *Kurt Schwitters: Space, Image, Exile.* Chicago: University of Chicago Press, 2014.

Man and His Symbols. Edited by Carl Jung and Marie Louise Von-Frantz, New York: Doubleday, 1964.

Montage, Satire and Cultism: Germany Between the Wars. Edited by Herbert Knust. Champaign, IL: University of Illinois Press, 1973.

Müller, Wolfgang. *Hausmusik Stare aus Hjertøya singen Kurt Schwitters.* Berlin: Wolfgang Müller and Galerie Katze 5 Röske & Schumacher GbR. 2000.

Parkin, Simon. *The Island of Extraordinary Captives.* New York: Simon & Schuster, 2022.

Rasula, Jed. *Destruction was My Beatrice: Dada and the Unmaking of the Twentieth Century.* New York: Basic Books, 2015.

Russell, John. *An Alternative Art*, The Meanings of Modern Art series, Vol. 6. New York: Museum of Modern Art, 1974.

Schmalenbach, Werner. *Kurt Schwitters*. New York: Abrams, 1967.

Schwitters, Kurt, Kocher, Ursula and Schulz, Isabel. *Band 4 Die Reihe Merz 1923–1932*, Berlin, Boston: De Gruyter, 2019. https://doi.org/10.1515/9783110624113

Schwitters, Kurt. *Kurt Schwitters. Die literarischen Werke*. Edited by Friedhelm Lach. Koln: Dumont, [1973] 1998.

Schwitters, Kurt. *Lucky Hans and other Merz Fairy Tales*. Translated by Jack Zipes. Princeton, NJ: Princeton University Press, 2009.

Schwitters, Kurt. Merz 24. Hannover: Merzverlag, 1932.

Schwitters, Kurt. *Merz Ecrits*. Paris: Editions Gerard Lebovici, 1990.

Schwitters, Kurt. *Myself and My Aims: Writings on Art and Criticism*. Edited by Megan Luke, translated by Timothy Grundy. Chicago, IL: University of Chicago Press, 2021.

Schwitters, Kurt. *PPPPPP: Poems Performances Pieces Proses Plays Poetics*. Edited by Jerome Rothenberg and Pierre Joris Philadelphia, PA: Temple University Press, 1993.

Schwitters, Kurt. *Three Stories, with a Tribute by E.L.T. Mesens*. Edited by Jasia Reichardt. London: Tate Publishing, 2010.

Schwitters, Kurt. *Wir Spielen bis uns die Tod abholt, Briefen aus Fünf Jahrzeiten*. Edited by Ernst Nündel. Franfurt/M: Verlag Ullstein, 1974.

Schwitters Miró Arp, edited by Dieter Buchhart. Munich: Prestel, 2016.

Steinitz, Kate Trauman. *Kurt Schwitters, A Portrait from Life.* Berkeley/Los Angeles, CA: University of California Press, 1968.

Stirton, Paul. *Jan Tschichold and the New Typography: Graphic Design Between the World Wars.* New Haven, CT: Yale University Press, 2019.

Text-Sound Texts. Edited by Richard Kostelanetz. New York: William Morrow, 1980.

Themerson Archive Catalog. Edited by Jasia Reichart and Nick Wadley. Boston, MA: MIT Press, 2020.

Themerson Stefan. *Kurt Schwitters in England.* London: Gaberbocchus Press, 1958.

Transition Workshop. Edited by Eugene Jolas. New York: Vanguard Press, 1949.

Webster, Gwendolen. *Kurt Merz Schwitters, A Biographical Study.* Cardiff: University of Wales Press, 1997.

Wilford, Hugh. *The Mighty Wurlitzer: How the CIA Played America.* Cambridge, MA: Harvard University Press, 2008.

World War 3 Illustrated: 1979-2014. Edited by Peter Kuper and Seth Tobocman. Binghamton, NY: PM Press, 2014.

INDEX

A

B

C

Cabaret Voltaire, 40, 101, 155
Capitalism, 43, 47, 48, 49
Carroll, Lewis, 28, 58
Cathedral of Erotic Misery, 80
Central Intelligence Agency, 45
Chagall, Marc, 20
Chicago Children's Museum, 47
Chicago Filmmakers, 21
Children's Bookstore, 47, 61, 91
Children's Museum Store, 91
Churchill, Winston, 45
Cinnabar, 29, 153
    Vermilion red, 28
Cleese, John, 19
Club Lower Links, 91
Clubhouse Studio, 98
Collage, 17
Coltrane, John, 74
Communism, 9, 22, 43, 45, 47, 48, 143, 150
Concannon, Kevin, 78
Congress for Cultural Freedom, 45
Constructivism, i
Corman, Ned, 13, 14
Creative Improvisers Orchestra, 82, 98, 163
Creative Music Studio, 98, 163, 166
Cubists, 24

D

dada, iii, 22, 25, 40, 61, 96, 149

Dada Invasion of West Haven, 65, 104, 160
Danz, Tracy, 49, 50
Das Grosse Lalula, 49, 156
Dedesnn nn rrrrr, 90
Degenerate Art, v, 10
Dickerson, Willard, 47, 48
Die Tödliche Doris, 33, 87
Die Zwiebel, 55
DJ Glove, 4, 6, 18, 66, 82, 94, 101, 102, 103
Dll rrrrrr beeeee bö, 49

E

Einstein, Albert, 24, 145
Eisenhauer, Lette, 96
Eisenhower, Dwight, 45
EkeEke ekeEke, 40
El Taller Latino Americano, 82
Electroluxopipophone, 4, 6
Elterwater Merz Barn, 17
Emit Gallery, 39
Epilepsy, 53, 54, 55, 86
Eric Carle Museum of Picture Book Art, 32
Ernst, Max, 20
Ewart, Douglas, 89

F

Fight Fascism!, 95
Final Fridays, 32, 33
Fineberg, Jonathan, 54
Fluxus, 18, 96
Fly, 52
fmsbwtözäu, 16
Forsberg, Josephine, 89
Fraktur, 9
Frankenstein, 74
Freud, Sigmund, 145

Kurt Schwitters (1887–1948) was a painter, collage-maker, typographer, sculptor, graphic designer, writer, and performer: one of the world's leading experimental artists.

Andrew Laties (1959–) co-founded Urchestra, Easton Book Festival, Book & Puppet Company, Vox Pop, The Children's Bookstore, Chicago Children's Museum Store, and Eric Carle Museum Bookstore. His *Ur Sonata* performances with Lynn Book were honored in the Museum of Contemporary Art's retrospective *Art in Chicago: 1945-1995*. He shared the 1987 Women's National Book Association's Pannell Award for bringing children and books together. His *Rebel Bookseller: Why Indie Businesses Represent Everything You Want to Fight For—From Free Speech to Buying Local to Building Communities* won the 2006 Independent Publisher Award and is available in a 2nd edition from Seven Stories Press.